Voice of the Ancestors VII

NFF: Never Forgive or Forget

Chase McGhee

Voice of the Ancestors

Voice of the Ancestors

CONTENTS

Voice of the Ancestors

Acknowledgement

Special thanks and acknowledgement to these special individuals for their love and support through this long process. For without you the creation of this book would have not been possible.

- Alegna Kween, London, U.K. (Editor)
- Precious Mmegwa, Nigeria
- Chantel Montague, Philadelphia, PA
- Chelsi Bender, New Jersey
- Tee, Sal, Cape Verde
- Ivory Mouzon, Georgia
- Britney Hull, New Orleans, LA
- De'Andrea Allen, Houston, TX
- Thurmond Gillis Jr, New Jersey
- Kyle Bailey, Atlanta, GA
- Joshua Patrick, Atlanta, GA
- Jacques Williams, Atlanta, GA
- Kelly Perry, Atlanta, GA
- Tajee Houston, Atlanta, GA
- Raymond McGhee, Atlanta, GA
- Colleen McGhee, Atlanta, GA
- Chanlor McGhee, Atlanta, GA
- Connie Raines, Conyers, GA
- Joel Mccandless, Birmingham, AL
- Joseph Wilson, Atlanta, GA
- Karesha Jones, Atlanta, GA
- Jimmy Lee Smith III, Rocky Mount, NC

- John Hall, Pollock Pines, CA
- Milton Duggins Jr., Tuscaloosa, AL
- Brianna Suber, Bryan, TX
- La'Darius Crutchfield, Ogden, UT
- Erika Warthen, Shelby, NC
- Nicholas Mason, Fayetteville, AR
- Rahsawn Hendricks, New Jersey
- Zonette Brown, Palm Spring, CA

Introduction

In my critically acclaimed and Amazon best-selling book, "Voice of the Ancestors Volume I", I discussed the idea of the black man and woman removing the shackles and chains from their mind. The reason being because, although many of us were set free physically in 1865, the slave mentality that was developed on the plantation, still remains alive and well in many African people till this day. This is a mentality that can only be fixed through the re-education process. Which is why we started off volume I of "Voice of the Ancestors", with a section entitled "Knowing Thy Self" and ended the book with a section entitled "L'Union Fait La Force", preaching how unity makes strength. Yet, it is important to note that if we truly want freedom and liberation for African people in America, breaking the shackles and chains off our mind isn't enough.

Because as history has shown us, it is not enough to get off one plantation, just to subscribe to the next one. It is not enough to scratch and claw your way to freedom, just to forgive those who denied it to you. It's not good enough to remember and honor everybody else's holocaust, just to forget your own. Which is why, after we have freed our minds from the slave mentality, we have to implement an NFF mentality. A mentality that teaches us to never forgive those who have done us wrong or forget the ancestors who came before us.

See, one of the biggest problems we have as African people, is that we are too forgiving and forgetting. As a result, we allow ourselves to fall into the same traps that we fell in before, freeing our mind temporarily just to put the shackles back on it later. Leading to the mental illnesses that we see today in our community, mainly in the form of

Stockholm Syndrome. A condition which causes African people to develop a psychological alliance with their captors during captivity and after, preventing us from taking our revolution to the next level as needed. We all know African people who suffer from Stockholm Syndrome.

These are members of the community who can be found often times, throwing out phrases such as, "black on black crime" or "we got to do better", whenever black people are harmed by each other. However, when our people are killed by the police or other white supremacist, you will hear the same people talk about forgiving and forgetting, like Botham Jean's family. Choosing to blame ourselves rather than the people who are harming us, or putting us in the conditions we are in. We are always pushing for self-accountability, but never for holding others accountable. This has to end.

No more forgiving our enemies or forgetting what they have done to our ancestors or their descendants. In this book, we will talk about the true history of slavery and the nation/empire that it built. Breaking down and exposing the European myths that are taught to us about the enslavement process of our Ancestors. Very important information to have, with reparation being a hot topic heading into the 2020 election. None the less, we will also shed light on life after slavery for African people in America, from Jim Crowism, to mass incarceration. Followed by the continued mental enslavement of African people through European culture and religion. Finishing it off with re-educating ourselves on the black woman, because as the great ancestor Dr. Yosef Ben Jochannan, once said "show me the condition of your woman, and I'll show you the condition of your people".

Therefore, it's a must that we discuss the role the

black woman has played in our history, as well as the pivotal role she must play in our liberation moving forward. In closing, let me answer a simple question I know some of you probably have on your mind, before moving on into the meat of the book. That question is "Chase, why in 2019 are we still talking about slavery or Jim Crowism? Why are we still talking about when our ancestors were at their lowest of the low, instead of when they were ruling the world as kings and queens?" These are all fair questions to ask, questions that I had when I came into consciousness.

However, as I continued to grow, I found out that the answer to these questions are simple. You see, the reason we must continue to remind ourselves of slavery, Jim Crowism, mass incarceration, or of our maafa as a whole, is because that's our "Why". Our "Why", gives us the balance, strength, and determination that we need on our path to liberation. Our "Why", is a constant reminder of the power we hold as a people, and what can happen if that power gets into the wrong hands. Our "Why", is the key to never letting anybody put shackles and chains on our body or mind ever again.

Just ask the European Jew why he has over 25 holocaust museums set up in the United States alone. Go ask the Japanese why they have a Hiroshima Peace Memorial set up in the middle of the city of Hiroshima. Better yet, next time you see some white folks down south; with some confederate flags hanging off their truck, ask them the reason for it. These people will tell you this is their "Why". A shining reminder for this generation and future generations to come, of who and what their fighting for and against. Because. as history has shown us, the weak give in and submit, while the strong never forgive or forget.

Chase McGhee

PART. 1

SLAVERY IN AMERIKKKA

"YOU SHOW ME THE DESCENDANTS OF AMERICAN SLAVES AND I WILL SHOW YOU WHY AMERICA IS THE ECONOMIC POWER IT IS TODAY"

-CHASE MCGHEE

Slavery, slavery, slavery it is the one thing Americans, especially white Americans, never seem to want to talk about. These same people will talk about black on black crime and black people being thugs and criminals all day, but as soon as you bring up slavery, everyone is quiet, or wants to brush over it. It is considered by most white historians and scholars, as America's dark past time. Yet whenever slavery is brought up, we the descendants of American slaves, are told to "get over it". We hear justifications like, "black people in America today were never enslaved, so why are we still talking about it".

Understand, this has always been a subject that has been a thorn in the side of white supremacist for years; because they know without the blood, sweat and tears, that came off the backs of our ancestors, there would be no America. Though we were supposedly set free on January 1, 1863 by the Emancipation Proclamation, we were only set free physically, never mentally. As a result, American descendants of slaves still suffer from the side effects of 400 years of enslavement. Therefore, in 2019 just like 1619, you still have house Negros and field Negros. The House negros have developed a mindset, that the white man or woman is not racist by nature, because they let them play for their team, or join their country club, or live in their neighborhood.

As a result, they will never call out racist actions against themselves or others, for fear of losing their spot in the house. Field Negros, on the other hand for the most part, are very aware of the racist ways of the white man and woman; yet deal with it in two different ways. The ways are either by trying to become a house negro to escape some of the brunt of the racism, or just by simply dealing with it and praying for better days. But, the average field negro unfortunately, will never rebel for fear they won't be able to survive. This is what I like to call the slave mentally, or the effects of slavery that many of us still have, but by no fault of our own.

You see, most American descendants of slaves just don't know, because they've never received any repair in the form of reparation, education or sociological help. We have been so dumbed down as a people, that now we are even allowing them to impute lies about how slavery wasn't even that bad. Nowadays, you will see a lot of these white supremacists attempt to normalize slavery by saying "well they had slavery in Africa" or "America is the only country that ever fought to end slavery" or my personal favorite, "the civil war was a form of reparations". This is why, in this chapter, we are going to debunk these myths, along with many others, to reveal the truth about slavery. As well as how our black labor, gave birth to white wealth here in the Americas. Because, the first step after you have removed the shackles and chains from your mind, is to never forget how they felt. For only then you can punish those responsible.

Myth#1
They kidnapped us all from Africa

Let's start at the beginning. Since grade school, we have been taught that every American slave came from Africa. However, this is not true as I revealed to you in Volume I, where I documented the presence of African people already here in America, prior to 1619. It was only upon the arrival of Christopher Columbus, and other European settlers, that the indigenous African people of America, were wiped out the history books, and put into shackles and chains and made slaves. Thousands upon thousands of African people, who were classified as Indians, were among the first slaves here in America. In the book "Africans and Native Americans", by Jack D. Forbes, he documents how many so called Native American Indians, were sold into slavery in Africa and Europe. This is the opposite direction in which we were taught the slave trade went in.

For example, Forbes points out in his book that Native Americans were always classified as Negros and Blacks in the slave books of Seville, Spain and elsewhere. On page 29 of "African and Native American" it says, "slaves from Terranova (Newfoundland), show up in the slave markets of Seville and Valencia very soon after the 1500's. For example, in Valencia during the early part of the 1500's to 1516, we find in 1503 Miguel, Manne, in 1505 Juan and Pedro, in 1507 Antonio and Juan Amarco, in 1515 Ali, now Melchor, in

1516 Catalina. They were all classified as Negro." Now that is very interesting isn't it? History has taught us over the years, that the first Africans were brought to north America to Jamestown, Virginia in 1619, and classified as slaves. However, we have documentation of Negro slaves being brought from America or the New World as early as the 1500's. This is supposedly more than 100 years before the so-called African men had ever stepped foot on north American soil.

Keep in mind as well, that one of the names of the native Americans, who were classified as a Negro, was "Ali." Now, what Indian do you know today named Ali? Ali is a dead giveaway that these were Moorish people, since Ali is a Moorish name. The slaves sold on the slave markets in the south, were initially African people from right here in America. This is why you see a constant effort of slave holding states, like Virginia, during the years of slavery, to deem Indians as slaves as well. Passing laws such as the Virginia law of 1682 and 1705 which deemed all Negros, Moors, Mulattos, and Indians, as slaves. Jack D. Forbes adds to this point in his book "Africans and Native Americans", saying, by the end of the colonial period, enslaved Indians were classified as Negro, along with their black enslaved counterparts.

Therefore, by the late 18th century, white settlers advocated for the state to stop recognizing Indian identity and territory, based on the idea that most Indians were Negros. To which, free native Americans, were classified on the census not as Indian, but as free people of color, or mulattoes. Also, to further the proof, Walter Plecker, former Virginia's Vital Statistics Registrar, once said, the Indians were nothing but "negros with feathers". With that being said, this does not mean that the African slave trade didn't exist, because there was indeed a kidnapping of Africans in

Africa, especially along the western coast. However, it was because of the mass shipment and slaughter of the Native people here in America, at the hands of Columbus and other European settlers.

Yet, this part of history always seems to be left out of our history books, and there is a very important reason for that. That is because the revealing of this information, would force the European powers that be, to rewrite the history books. All of that "Columbus founded America" nonsense, would be forced out the window, due to the fact that a small percentage of black slaves in America were indigenous to the land. This is why, according to Journals like "Canada: The Promised Land for U.S. Slaves" by Reese Renford, they estimated as many as 100,000 slaves escaped to freedom during the time of slavery, up until the civil war. How is this, if we didn't already know the layout of the land?

Look at some of our ancestors, like queen mother Harriet Tubman, who knew the layout of the land like the back of her hand. Many escaped slaves were known to go up into the mountains, or to the swamps, like The Great Dismal, to evade Europeans who could not maneuver the land to find them. Also, many-escaped slaves would make their way back to tribes down south, in places like Florida, such as the Seminoles. This was one of the biggest reasons white supremacists felt the need to implement the Fugitive Slave Act of 1850, increasing the penalties against fugitive slaves and people who aided them. Africans were already indigenous to the land; this is why a good proportion were able to escape. Because remember, most of us did not know how to read or write the English language, so it was not like we had written directions, we just knew the land.

See, the dominant white society can live with saying that the Indians, with the Mongolian phenotype, who are lighter complexioned, and still pertain Asiatic features, are the indigenous people of the land. This helps with the white supremacist psyche. Yet they refuse to admit the obvious; that a small proportion of black people who were enslaved, were in fact indigenous to America; because that would break down their whole superiority complex, as well as make them and everybody else ask the question, how long have they been here?

Paintings from Louis Choris of Native Americans from Hawaii to San Francisco to the Carolinas, 1816 - 1822

Echolovonis a la chasse dans la baie de St. Francisco, 1822 - 1825

Habitans des iles Sandwich, 1816

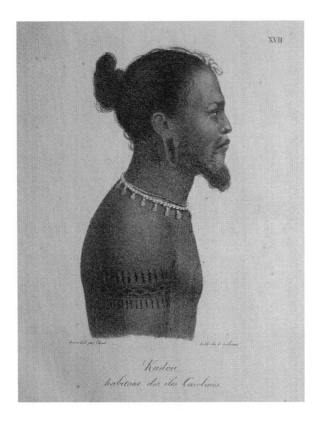

'Kadou, habitant des îles Carolines', 1822

Myth#2
Slavery in America was the same as slavery of the past

One of the most common and most popular arguments among white supremacists is "there was slavery everywhere throughout history, just like in America". I always find this to be one of the funnier argument points of them all, from the sheer stupidity of it. Let's deal with the facts. Firstly yes, it is true that slavery is one of the oldest forms of trade known to man. All races and all civilizations have practiced a form of slavery at one point in time or another. From

China to India to Europe to America and yes, even Africa. Black, White, Hispanic, native American etc. have all engaged in the system of slavery.

However, it is important to note that human beings, in both ancient and modern times, were rarely randomly enslaved. Normally enslaved individuals or groups were enslaved as a result of personal debt, religious differences, or as punishment stemming from war. Arabs enslaved the Mongolians, who in return enslaved the Chinese and the Russians. The Hebrews enslaved and were enslaved by the Egyptians. Victorious Roman and Greek armies conquered the Mediterranean area and made slaves of the nations and their people, regardless of race ethnicity, or color.

In fact, slavery became so common in ancient Roman times, that Roman laws focused on protecting the slave's humanity and basic rights during the temporary enslavement period. The Catholic church would even do its part to intervene on behalf of the slave, to make sure their rights were upheld. In the same Latin American societies, due to the Catholic church, some slaves were even able to win their freedom in court, with compensation from cruel slave masters. In more simple terms, in ancient times, the Catholic church and Roman law, gave the enslaved some options and basic protections. Even slavery in Africa was similar to that of Rome in a sense.

You see, European scholars and historians alike, love to bring up the fact that there was slavery in Africa. As if it justifies the enslavement of Africans in America by Europeans. Truth is yes, slavery in Africa did exist, but it was similar to most Ancient forms of slavery; where a person might be enslaved, in order to pay off a debt or to pay for a crime. This sounds much like the criminal justice system we have in America today that so many white Americans seem to love. The treatment of slaves in Africa varied widely on many different scales.

Ottobah Cuguano, for example, who was an African Abolitionist and natural rights Philosopher, said he remembered African slaves being, "well fed and having good care taken of them, and treated well". Olaudah Equiano, who was also an Abolitionist, noted that African slaves might even have slaves of their own. Of course, I'm not trying to make the impression, or paint a picture, that slavery in other parts of the world and in other time periods throughout history, was heaven on earth. However, it must be noted that it was heaven, compared to America's form of slavery. You see, they try to use that "it was slavery everywhere", as a cop out. A way to justify the atrocity they made others endure.

Yet that was far from the case. Enslavement in America was unique in nearly every aspect, from any previous known instinct of human enslavement or serfdom. Some of you might be thinking how is slavery different? I mean slavery is slavery, right? Wrong, we as Africans in America, endured what is known as chattel slavery.

Chattel slavery means we were just a piece of property. You as a person of African descent, were just considered three-fifths of a human being. Do you realize that they did not even consider us a whole person in America? Rather, a monkey or ape that could be used and worked as one. Now compare that to enslaved people elsewhere throughout history, who were not only considered a person, but who also had rights to make sure you treated them as such. Which is why other forms of slavery don't compare to ours.

First thing that made chattel slavery unlike any other slavery in history was the sheer size of it. According to Dr. Claud Anderson, in the book "Black Labor White Wealth", an estimated 15 to 60 million slaves, were captured in Africa for enslavement. As well as, an estimated more than 35 million, died en route to various ports, with approximately 15 million, actually reaching the slave markets. Yes, you heard me correctly, as many as 35 million died en route to various slave ports to the Americas. Let's stop for a second and put that into context. During the Nazi Regime in Germany, an estimated five to six million Jews were killed.

This was a horrible event that took place, an atrocity that still has an effect on the Jewish community to this day. However, it is downright disrespectful and a spit in the face for the United States of America to go out of its way to build several Holocaust Memorial museums, when they have still yet to build a museum honoring our African ancestors, who were murdered and pillaged of their home land during slavery. Do you see the irony in that, when an estimated 6 times as many Africans died then in the Jewish-German Holocaust? Remember this, 35 million is just the estimated number of those of us that died in route to the slave markets. Now add that to the millions of the indigenous Africans of this land who were murdered, captured, and pillaged of their god given land and rights.

Remember, our Holocaust wasn't just 2 to 3 years, but 2 to 3 hundred years. Yet people have the nerve to tell African people to get over slavery but wouldn't dare tell a Jew to get over the holocaust. These people have lost their mind. But wait we are not done. The second thing that made slavery in the Americas different, is that it was the only slavery in history, that was purely racial. No other slavery in history, were people enslaved based purely on their racial profile.

Other racial groups, especially whites, love to bring up the fact that Black Muslims used to enslave white people. Again, yes this is true, but we must also note that you as white people, were not enslaved because of your skin color, but because you were a prisoner of war or religious misbeliefs. In our case, anybody who had black skin, was subjected to enslavement, no matter what he or she had done. Black people were enslaved, simply because they were black. When European bodies came to Africa, it became known they were looking for, and seeking out, strong melanated bodies.

Subsequently, black skin color became a sign of degradation for its wearer, and a sign of wealth for people who did not obtain it. Third thing that made American slavery different from anywhere else, is that those who were enslaved, were forced to practice the religion of their master. Which is why in most, if not all cases in America, Christianity was the religion of choice. Slave owners used Christian principles to promote the belief that, people with black skin owed an unpaid debt to people with pale skin. A debt that could only be paid through perpetual bondage.

In the book "Black Labor White Wealth" it states that, "West African blacks never left their African Continent to go to war with another nation. There was no known organized effort of African people to impose their religions on white societies and there is no recorded balance of payments that were due to the European nations, as a result of any trade relation with Black Africa. The same could not be said for any of the European nations, which routinely sent armies to engage in warfare, to promote Christian religions and conduct exploitative trade with other nations". Fourth thing that made America's chattel slavery unique from any other, is the simple fact that a slave could be killed for attempting to learn how to read or write. Most of the time, only a select few slaves were picked out the bunch to learn any form of education, whether it be reading or writing. The only purpose of that in most cases, was to further push the notion of Christianity on other members of the slave population. This for example is the only reason that some of our great ancestors, like Nat Turner, were taught how to read.

Fear from Cato's rebellion in 1740, caused mass panic among slave owners, which caused Carolina to pass the first law prohibiting slave education in 1740. Education of slaves was generally discouraged, from the fear that knowledge and literacy would cause rebelliousness. States like Virginia punished violators of slave educational law, with twenty lashes to the slave and a fine of a hundred dollars to the teacher. North Carolina's punishment for teaching a slave, was thirty-nine lashes to the slave and a two hundred-fifty dollar fine to the teacher. These lashes could result in serious injuries or even death.

Slaves could also even be sold away from their family, with the thought that education would make them a threat to rise up and rebel against the dominant white society. This type of mistreatment of slaves was unheard of throughout history. Even slavery in ancient times, you were allowed to try to learn. In fact, slaves in Ancient Rome were highly educated, judging by the fact that some were, accountants and physicians, because in most cases they were slaves of war. Moving on, last but not least, American slavery was the only slavery in history that pushed mass breeding of slaves.

In 1807, the British put into place the slave trade act of 1807, which abolished slave trade in the British Empire. In particular, the Atlantic slave trade. This law took effect in 1808, which was permitted by the United States constitution. This in return caused white American slave owners, to be faced with a major dilemma. How are they going to keep growing their native slave population without any new slaves being brought in? The answer they came up with, was the mass breeding of African slaves.

Now, slaves were always encouraged to have a lot of babies to keep their masters happy. The reason being, that slaves were only considered as three-fifths of a human being, nothing more than property. The white supremacists looked at newborn babies as if they were stocks to improve their overall slave portfolio. Thus, seeing them as new assets, that could be sold or worked for profit, free of charge. However, after the slave trade act of 1807, slave breeding, more than ever, became big business in the United States.

Professor Smithers Gregory explains greatly in his book "Slave Breeding, Sex, Violence, and Memory in African American History", there was a mass breeding of African slaves in this country after the year 1807 that is rarely talked about. African scholar W.E.B. DuBois, states during the turn of the 19th century, the enslaved population was roughly around or just over a million enslaved Africans. However, on the eve of the Civil War, the slave population stood at a little over four million. In between that time, we saw an increase of 20 to 30 percent over the next five to six decades, according to Professor Gregory Smith. Now, keep in mind this is occurring after the abolishment of the international slave trade by the United States in 1808.

Now of course, there is still some smuggling of slaves into the boarders, but a majority of that rise of the population, however, is through natural increase, in the case of breeding farms. Two of the largest slave breeding farms in the United States were on the eastern shore of Maryland and right outside of Richmond, Virginia. On these two breeding farms, they literally bred African slaves like cattle. They would force young healthy fertile women to have sex with the biggest and strongest males. When enslaved males turned 15 or sometimes younger, they were first inspected by the slave master. If these boys were under-developed, they would have their testicles castrated and sent to the market or they were to be used strictly for the farm.

Each enslaved male was expected to get 12 or more females pregnant a year. The men were used for breeding for 5 years. One enslaved man named Burt, produced more than two hundred offspring, according to the "Slave Narratives". As well, according to the book "Slavery in the United States" by John Simkin, plantation owners demanded females start having children at thirteen, and by age twenty, they would be expected to have four or five children. As an inducement, plantation owners promised freedom for enslaved females once she bore fifteen children.

To make matters even worse, on these breeding farms, the main goal was to produce more assets in the form of children to be sold off or kept as capital. It did not matter if they had to mate a mother and son, daughter and father, or brother and sister. As long as they produced children. Let's be clear, no form of slavery in history, has these types of inhumane acts been forced on a group of people, especially on such a large scale in which it creates a business and country. These are five facts that distinguish American slavery from any other slavery known to man.

These are just five. I could have named many more, yet for now, all I want you to remember are these five facts. Facts that separate the African Holocaust in America from any other. So, the next time someone tells you "slavery in America was the same as any other slavery throughout history". Respond back with these simple words "Child Please"!

Myth#3
Slavery did not have anything to do with America's rise to Economic Power

A common lie many white supremacists and other anti-black groups like to tell is, slavery was not that profitable and contributed nothing to America's economic rise. Contrary to popular beliefs or myths, prior to the Civil War the south was not poverty stricken but held the greatest concentration of per capita wealth in the nation. This was the whole reason for the Civil War. See, we as American Descendants of slaves are taught in school to believe that the north is where the good white folks were, and they did not agree or associate themselves with slavery. When facts are white folks in the north had no problem at all with slavery, because history shows us that most of their goods were manufactured by slaves in the south.

The truth is, the sole reason for the Civil war, was for the simple fact that the south was growing too powerful due to slavery. It was never because they cared about African slaves one way or another. After all, some of the first stocks sold on wall street were slaves. Slaves in fact built the wall that gave Wall Street its famous name. Numerous historians such as Stanley Lebergott, E.N. Elliott, and Robert Fogel, document the massive amounts of wealth slave labor produced for the north. For example, by 1850 more than 1,000 cotton factories operated in the United States. Northern Mills processed one quarter of all slave produced cotton. Leading to clothes, fabric, jobs, income, wealth, taxes, and other benefits to the white population throughout the north.

Yet somehow this never ends up in our history books. All of America, both north and south, benefited heavily from slavery. Slaves in the south could be used as monetary exchanges that could be bartered or accepted as collateral, when currency or other valuables were in short supply. Making it where a white slave owner always had opportunity, since he could use his slaves as human capital. The book "Black Labor White Wealth", states that the average value of a slave in the late 1700's was about 400 to 500 dollars for a field slave. Nearly a half century later on the eve of the civil war, field slaves were priced right around 1,600 to 1,800 dollars.

Meaning just like stocks, the value of a slave appreciated over time, creating long term wealth for its owners. Land ownership in America, which was the second greatest tool to white wealth, did not surpass slave ownership as the primary form of wealth accumulation until well after the civil war. In fact, slavery was so profitable at the time, that anything short of the civil war would have had little effect on the system of slavery here in the United States. The 7-billion-dollar capital investments in black slaves in 1860, exceeded all other businesses and federal budget combined. As a result, many of the world's wealthiest families today, money links back to slavery.

Cornelius Vanderbilt, part of the Vanderbilt family considered to be one of the richest families in the world, was a tycoon who built his wealth from shipping and railroads. However, they never tell you that he owned several slave plantations as well. Thomas Walker is another notorious vicious slave trader, who became very wealthy making at least two slave voyages to West Africa between 1784 and 1792. Thomas Walker happens to be a direct ancestor of George W. and George H.W. Bush. Senate Majority Leader Mitch McConnell, who opposed the notion in early 2019 of paying government reparations to American descendants of slaves, comes from a lineage of slave owners. McConnell's two great-great-grandfathers, James McConnell and Richard Daley, owned a total of at least 14 slaves in Limestone County, Alabama; all but two of them female, according to the county "Slave Schedules" in the 1850 and 1860 censuses.

To put that in perspective, those 14 slaves valued at $1,600 a piece according to market prices of the time, would have given the family an equivalent of $700,000 in today's money and remember, that's just in slave labor alone. These are just to name a couple of people. There are many big names who have family ties leading all the way back to slavery, Richard Dawkins, Paula Dean, John McCain, etc. Many public institutions as well, were a part of the slave trade, one being Georgetown University. Georgetown University is considered one of the top Universities as far as history is concerned, in the United States.

However, up until recently Georgetown always seemed to leave out the part about its history of slavery. In 1838 Georgetown University sold off 272 slaves to pay a debt. Let me repeat that number one more time in case you missed it "272". The "272" slaves were sold for about $115,000, which would be about 3.2 million dollars today. This is money that ultimately ended up saving the university. Families were separated as a result and many were sent down to sugar plantations in the south.

Yale University, another nationally recognized school, used profit from a plantation that was donated to them by Bishop George Berkeley, to fund their first scholarships. Some of Harvard University's first donors had connection to slavery, such as one Isaac Royall Jr., whose family were notorious slave traders out of the West indies. It was Isaac Royall Jr's, generous land donation that helped Harvard establish a Chair in Law, making him the first Law Professorship at Harvard. Financial intuitions like Lehman Brothers, and business empires started in the slave trade. According to the National Public Radio, the financial services firms acknowledged recently that its founding partners owned not one, not two, but several enslaved Africans during the Civil War era and that, it "profited significantly from slavery".

Harvard Law unveiled a memorial for slaves who made it possible

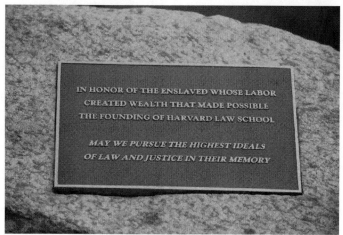

IN HONOR OF THE ENSLAVED WHOSE LABOR
CREATED WEALTH THAT MADE POSSIBLE
THE FOUNDING OF HARVARD LAW SCHOOL

*MAY WE PURSUE THE HIGHEST IDEALS
OF LAW AND JUSTICE IN THEIR MEMORY*

New York Life was also involved in slavery. The insurance company is one of the largest mutual fund companies in the United States today. They sold insurance policies on enslaved Africans, according to USA Today, evidence of at least ten or more New York slave policies came from an 1847 account book kept by the companies, Natches, Miss. Agent, and WA. Britton. A 1906 history of New York Life, says 339 of the company's first 1,000 policies, were written on the lives of slaves. It's funny, I referenced the USA Today talking about how New York Life had ties to slavery, because they did too.

The USA today has found that their own parent company, E.W. Scripps and Gannet, had links to the slave trade. The fact is, all of the institutions I mentioned above, including Rutgers, Brown, University of Virginia, JP Morgan Chase, Aetna Inc and more, were all in some way or form, heavily involved in the business of slavery. Also keep in mind, most of these corporations and institutions were located in the north. This is key, because as I said before, the north always gets a pass when it comes to slavery. All in all, the dream of living in the New World, with unlimited free land and economic opportunities to many impoverished whites in Europe and elsewhere, was made possible off the backs of our enslaved African ancestors. Even whites who did not directly benefit from slavery by owning slaves, benefited indirectly by owning businesses and supporting farms that sustained themselves by buying and selling slave produced products.

Businesses supporting plantations generated massive income for the community. These slave dollars in return, help to create jobs and provide work for many whites, even establishing and sustaining towns such as Charleston, Savannah, Norfolk and New Orleans. These opportunities provided by slave labor were so great, that many European whites were willing to sell or contract their labor, just to get a chance to enjoy the fruits of America created by slave labor. These people were known as white indentured servants and their labor was only temporary. White America made all types of deals to get their white immigrant brothers and sisters to travel from all over, in order to participate in Black exploitation.

For example, to increase land utilization, some states, like North and South Carolina, granted free land to white settlers simply for owning slaves. In 1663, the British Lords Proprietors offered additional acreage for every male and female slave brought into Carolina during the first 5 years of white settlement. Which created a massive amount of wealth and land ownership for whites, which still holds true today. So, as you can see, the dream of owning slaves and land, which drew white settlers to America and liberated them from federal oppression in Europe, turned out to be an African nightmare. It smothered black's dreams by shackling them into endless human exploitation. Thus, building an unrivaled economic power through slavery, which provided the corner stone for wealth here in America.

Myth#4
Chattel Slavery was only in the United States

Most of the time, we are taught just about the enslaved Africans who were captured and brought to the United States. However, it is well documented that not only was there slavery in South America and many of the islands; it was considered by many scholars and historians worse than slavery in the states. An estimated more than 90 percent of slaves arriving from Africa, were shipped to South America and the Caribbean islands. Only about 4 to 6 percent of Africans were sent or arrived directly in the United States. This puts this estimate at around 388,000 enslaved Africans having landed here in the United States, between 1525 and 1866.

Remember, this is just the number that is believed to have actually made it, millions of millions died in the journey over. However, in this same period, as many as 4.86 million enslaved Africans were in Brazil alone.

J.B. Derbet, "Overseers punishing slaves on a rural estate"

This would explain the overwhelming population of Africans that are still in Brazil today. As we discussed earlier in Volume I of Voice of the Ancestors, Brazil has the largest population of Africans outside of Africa. The slave trade is the biggest reason for that.

These African slaves and their descendants, were Brazil's dominant population until the mass influx of Europeans into Brazil, arriving in the late 19th century. This was long after slavery had been terminated and European wealth and power had amassed due to the fruits created by forced black labor in that country. As well, just like Africans in the states, African Brazilians are still excluded from enjoying the fruits and are gunned down in the streets by death squads. Slavery in the Caribbean islands was no different. The economics of the Caribbean Islands were similar to North, South, and Central America. In the Caribbean, black labor spawned numerous cottage industries that provided many resources for European trade such as sugar, tobacco, molasses, vinegar, rum etc.

In most cases, African slaves were at least sold twice before reaching their destination and produced an incredible amount for slave traders in South America and the West Indies or Caribbean. Places where the average price drew around $500 a slave. Multiply that by the ten to 15 million slaves that arrived as a result, giving these places a trillion-dollar economy. This is money that eventually trickled back up to Europe, seeming that most of these slave holding countries were colonies of European nations such as France and England. Places like the Caribbean also served as seasoning plantations for slaves.

Seasoning plantations were put together to take and strip the enslaved Africans of all knowledge of one's self and prepare them for lifelong servitude. At the seasoning farms, the enslaved were put under many forms of torture. Having already been branded once in Africa or whichever land they came from. They would be branded a second time by their new owners, who would also give them a Christian name. African practices and customs of religious would begin to become discouraged. Some of the enslaved population already weakened by the horrors of the voyage, committed suicide while on the seasoning farms. Others died under the pressures of the farms.

They would also break the mental ties between the African men and women. The white slave owners of these seasoning plants would tie the male slaves up and exploit them sexually. To these white supremacists, this was a way for them to show dominance over the African men, similar to the way a male dog humps another male dog to show dominance. This is the reason today, if you visit most islands in the Caribbean, like Jamaica for example, they are very hard on homosexuality. These were normal practices to take the mind, body, and soul away from the slave. Thus, when they arrived on their permitted plantation rather on the islands and or the states, they would be nothing more than a body.

Myth#5
The Scared and Passive African Slave

Oftentimes, enslaved African people are portrayed in the media today as scared and passive people. We rarely hear about the times we resisted and when we stood our ground. They try to make us believe that we were just laying around getting beat, praying for some white Jesus to come save us. However, this was not the case, most of us know about Nat Turner and Harriet Tubman and how they resisted and fought for our freedom. The mainstream always attempts to act as if our ancestors, such as Turner and Tubman were isolated incidents, yet they were not.

We have always resisted our enslavement and exploitation, going all the way back to Africa. Many of our West African brothers and sisters resisted enslavement, even when confronted by the collective military and economic might of Portugal, Spain, Germany, England and the Arab nations. Of the estimated tens of millions of Africans believed to be captured and shipped out of Africa, it is believed that most ships never reached the slave markets. Contrary to popular belief, most slaves were killed resisting their oppressors or just flat out jumping the ship to avoid the inhumane conditions. Knowing that they would rather die fighting their oppressors or at the hands of the sea, than to spend a lifetime in bondage.

For example, on July 2, 1839, fifty-two Africans took over the LA Amistad; a ship embarking from Havana, on a journey to bring valuables and slaves to trade, killing the captain, cook and three of the crew members. The slaves demanded to be taken back to Africa, but unfortunately were tricked into continuing to the United States by the two white passengers they kept alive to guide the boat. Once the ship landed in New York, the slaves were arrested and transported to Connecticut for trial. However, the revolt on the LA Amistad created a massive national political drama, that resulted in the first anti-slavery decision proclaimed before the United States Supreme Court in 1841. The LA Amistad is just one of the more well-known uprisings that occurred.

There are others such as the Creole Ship Uprising, the Little George Ship Revolt, Captain Beers, overtaken in West Africa, Captain John Major of Portsmouth, N.H killings, and more. You even have historic sites such as the Igbo landing at Dunbar Creek on St. Simons Island in Glynn County Georgia. A place that was the setting of a mass suicide in 1803 by captive Igbo people who had taken control of their slave ship. Yet rather than choosing to be re-enslaved, some decided in unison to enter a nearby creek singing in the Igbo language "The Water Spirit brought us, the Water Spirit will take us home", thereby accepting the protection of their god Chukwu and death over the bondage of slavery.

Igbo Landing

This is just one of many courageous rebellions our ancestors undertook against their oppressors on the seas. The truth is, roughly 15 to 20 percent of the ship that left Africa, never made it to the "New World". Thousands of vessels were overtaken by the enslaved Africans on board. These enslaved African men and women sometimes rose up and killed every white man on the ship or forced them to sail them back from where they came. There are cases as well, when slave ship uprising would happen. The enslaved African's would take over the ship and return back to Africa and tell the people what abuses they were facing.

Queen Nzingha of Angola was one of our African Queens who fought and stood up for African people. Queen Nzingha fought a successful 30-year war against the slave traders of Portugal, until the Portuguese negotiated a treaty with her in 1656. Their treaty remained in effect until she died in 1663. Even today in Angola, Queen Nzingha is remembered for her political and diplomatic acumen, as well as her brilliant military tactics. Today among the Angolan people, she is considered a symbol of the fight against oppression. Queen Nzingha also has a major street in Lunda named after her, as well as a statue of her placed in Kinaxixi.

Queen Nzingha was just one of the many. Another was the Senegal King of Almammy, who in 1787 passed a law that made it illegal to take enslaved Africans through his kingdom. To let Europeans, know how serious the law of the land was, the King returned the presents French slave traders sent as bribes. Many countries resisted, such as Senegal, Ghana, Benin, Nigeria, Angola and more. In fact, most of the history about African resistance against European enslavement, was well documented by European sailors. Historians try to make it seem as if all African Kings and Queens were ok with the enslavement of their people. However, that was far from the truth.

Enslavement was never universally accepted among African people. Most African rulers like King Ansah of Ghana would not even allow Europeans on his land. As a result, King Ansah had the Fente people watch for European ships, in order to prevent them from coming ashore. In Benin, the people there, heard about the intentions of the Europeans, so they killed them as soon as they came ashore. The slaves that were caught and survived the trip to the Americas from Africa, also resisted as well. As I stated before, many of us know about Nat Turner's Rebellion, but many of us don't know that there was an estimated 150 to 200 organized slave rebellions.

One of which being the New York Slave revolt of 1712. Where twenty-three enslaved Africans killed nine people and injured six more. Determined to gain their freedom, they also set fire to a building on Maiden Lane near Broadway, where they waited for colonists to come to put the flames out and then proceeded to attack them. One of the main reasons they never talk about the New York Slave Revolts of 1712 is because of the location in which it took place. The North.

I warned you all earlier, about how the north gets a pass in slavery. They try to hide this revolt to save face. Just another lie we are told, so white people in the north can feel better about themselves; but we're going to expose the truth. Before we get deeper into that, let's get back to the lecture at hand on African slave resistances. Because it's important we understand that not only did those who were enslaved rebel, but free Africans too, in order to free their brothers and sisters from bondage.

Many of us don't know about a man named Denmark Vesey, who was a freeman and leader amongst African Americans in Charleston, South Carolina in 1822. Vesey was the accused and convicted ringleader of "the rising", a major potential slave revolt planned for Charleston, South Carolina. However, before they could spring the revolt, he was told on by one of his own men, as a result he was executed. It is believed by many historians that if the revolt had been carried out, it could have possibly been the biggest slave revolt in American history. Gabriel's Rebellion was another revolt that never panned out like Vesey's, but their spirit of rebellion lived on.

Many others, like the New York Revolt of 1712, did indeed pan out. For example, the store Rebellion, the German coast uprising, the New York Slave insurrection of 1741 and more. Some never got classified as slave rebellions at all, even though they were. Rebellions like the Seminole Wars that often get reclassified as strictly a war between whites and Indians, when in fact it was undoubtedly a negro war. When the first Seminole war, or sometimes known as Florida war, broke out in 1812, it was led by General Andrew Jackson, who later became the 7th president of the United States. Interesting enough, when looking back on his accounts of the war, he always referred to it as an "Indian and Negro War".

To add to that in 1835, when the Second Seminole War broke out, and this full-scale guerrilla war, would last for 6 years and claim the lives of 1,500 American soldiers. During this time, the American Commander, General Jesup, informed the War Department that, "This, you may be assured, is a negro and not an Indian war"; and a U.S. Congressman of the period commented that these black fighters were, "contending against the whole military power of the United States." As a result, when the Army finally captured the Black Seminoles, officers refused to return them to slavery, fearing that these seasoned warriors, accustomed to their freedom, would wreak havoc on the southern plantations.

John Horse, Black Seminole Warrior

Yet these rebellions in our history are left out. As well, it is important to note when speaking of rebelling, that just because slaves weren't picking up weapons and attacking white folks, doesn't mean they weren't rebelling. For instance, some rebel slaves just impeded the work process by breaking work tools, feigning illnesses, running away or refusing to work or eat. Some also fought for their freedom and revenge by poisoning and setting the big house or the whole plantation on fire. According to the book "Black Labor White Wealth" There were so many incidents of poisoning, that many states passed laws prohibiting blacks from working in and around drug stores or supplies.

These were more common forms of resisting for African slaves. There were also rebellions outside of the United States, the most popular and most successful of them all was the Haitian Revolution. The Haitian Revolution is an event that is never discussed in our history or any other culture's history for that matter. The reason being the mainstream media does not want you to know about the times when we fought back and won. Haiti is a shining example of that. Haiti is the only nation in the western hemisphere in which the native slave population rose up and took over.

This revolution became a major thorn in the side of western powers, even up until today. This is the reason why now, just like back then, they purposely sabotage Haiti through trade sanctions etc. White supremacists are still mad that a group of enslaved African people who they claimed to be inferior to whites, defeated some of the biggest western powers, to gain their freedom and independence. The Haitian Revolution lasted from 1791 to 1804, where enslaved Africans succeeded in ending not just slavery, but French control over the colony as well. What made the Haitian revolution different than many of the other slave revolts throughout the Americas, was not only the fact that it was successful, but the complexity of the revolution. At the time, before the revolution, Saint Domingue and Haiti were known as one of France's wealthiest overseas colonies.

Wealth that had been generated by the enslaved African labor force who produced the sugar, coffee, and cotton that made the French colony so profitable. Even before the start of the Haitian revolution, due to the brutal treatment and conditions of the Haitian Slave, which saw their average life span last only 21 years, there were many slave revolts. All leading to the major revolution starting in 1791. With numbers on their side similar to slavery in America, a lot of rebellions started with the poisoning of the plantation owner or things of that sort. However, the French revolution led to the birth of the Haitian revolution. This caused many Haitian revolutionary movements to emerge all at once, inspired by the "Declaration of the Rights of Man".

The Declaration was initially a three-sided civil war between the planters, free blacks and the petit Blancs, who were like the working-class citizens of Saint Dominique. However, all three groups would be challenged by the enslaved African majority, which was also influenced by the Declaration of France. Thus by 1792, these enslaved Africans led by Toussaint L' Overture, had controlled more than a third of the island. Despite troops being sent in from France, who was a major world power at the time. The area held by the rebels grew, as did the violence on both sides. Before all of the fighting had ended, it is estimated that as many as 100,000 blacks and 24,000 whites were killed.

Nonetheless, the former slaves managed to fight off the French forces. They also fought off the British force who arrived in 1793 to try and conquer the colony, but eventually withdrew in 1798. It is important to note that the Haitian's after abolishing slavery, did not just stop there. By 1801, Toussaint L'Ouverture expanded the revolution beyond

Haiti, conquering the neighboring Spanish colony of Santo Domingo, which is now present-day Dominican Republic. Toussaint L'Ouverture abolished slavery in Santo Domingo and declared himself Governor-General for life, over the entire island of Hispaniola.

Not over yet, the French gave it one last try. Napoleon Bonaparte, the ruler of France at the time, dispatched 43,000 French troops to capture L'Ouverture. Unfortunately, L'Ouverture was captured and taken back to France, where he died in prison in 1803. Yet, the spirit of revolution continued to live on. His replacement was Jean-Jacques Dessalines, who was one of L'Ouverture's Generals, as well as a slave himself.

He was also the inspiration behind the Nat Turner Rebellion, which Nat later stated himself upon his capture. Dessalines led the revolution on at the Battle of Vertieres on November 18, 1803, where the French forces were defeated, leading to the January 1, 1804 declaration of Saint Domingue independence and renaming it to Haiti. Haiti thus emerged as the first black republic in the world and the second nation in the western hemisphere, only behind the United States, to win its' independence from a European power. Haiti also became well known for accepting runaway slaves from North America, as well as other slave nations or islands, giving them a safe haven to stay. It comes as a surprise to many European scholars and historians on how they were able to achieve this massive military feat.

One of the biggest reasons for the Haitian's success that is never talked about, is their belief in voodoo. The Haitian people made up their mind that they were not going to keep praying to some white Jesus and wait for him to come save us them.

The Haitian Revolution. Slave rebellion on the night of 21 August 1791, 1805. Private Collection. Artist Rainsford, Marcus

They stopped believing the lies of their oppressors. Lies such as, if they were a good slave, they might go to heaven. They stopped believing in a religious system rooted in white supremacy, that taught them to obey your master, even when he is beating the hell out of you. Our Haitian ancestors went back to their original African spirituality system of voodoo. The same voodoo that teaches you that when white supremacists shoot at you, you shoot back, and when they hit you, you hit them back.

This is why voodoo today, has always been seen and depicted as devil like behavior within the western media outlets. The French saw voodoo as a forbidden dance and religion or a form of devil worshiping. As well, the French tried their best to keep the Haitian Slaves from practicing it, yet the voodoo prevailed. As a vital spiritual force, voodoo was a source of physical liberation, in that it enabled them to express a form of rebellion against their oppressors. Voodoo further allowed the enslaved Africans of Haiti, to break away psychologically, from the very mental and physical chains of slavery and to see themselves as independent beings.

Returning to their original African spirituality, enabled them to find a way to feel human in order to survive. Voodoo will always be seen in a demonic form because again, we are looking at it through the European eyes of the western media. Yet it is the spiritual system that enabled us to break free of our enslavement, Christianity on the other hand, put us in it. This is something we will discuss more in part three, when we go deep on religion. All in all, as you can see, there was no such thing as a submissive slave.

We were never satisfied with our position in America or abroad. Many of our ancestors fought and died to be free. From the kings and queens of Africa, to the Maroons of Jamaica, all the way to freeman right here in America who had everything to lose but very little to gain. So, in the words of the WBC heavyweight champion of the world Deontay Wilder just know, "our people have been fighting 400 years and are still fighting till this day".

Myth#6
Slavery was a long time ago

Whenever African people anywhere in the world, bring up any matter regarding receiving restitution or reparations for our African Holocaust, the first response we receive as it pertains to slavery, is that it was a long time ago. Well my brothers and sisters, I am here to tell you that is an illusion to continue to put time between the past and the present. An illusion and arguing point that can be debunked rather quickly. First point and fact are that African people have been slaves in this country longer than we have been free. Do the math yourself if you don't believe me.

According to European history books, they state that slavery began in 1619 in the 13 colonies and ended in 1865. Now we know, as I have stated before in this book, it started much earlier than that. However, we will go by their date. Putting two and two together, we were enslaved a total of 246 years here in the United States of America. However, we have only been so called free, 154 years.

Thus, we still have nearly 100 years left till we are free for as long as we were enslaved. Which means that most American descendants of slavery are only five or six generations removed from slavery. When you think about it from a historical standpoint, that's not that long, considering the average person most of the time, lives through about three generations. Take me for example, my great grandmother Laura Gordon, who I knew and spent time with as a kid in Mississippi. Her grandmother, who is my great, great, great grandmother Fannie Springfield, was a slave. Meaning I had direct connection with someone who knew someone personally that was enslaved.

All in all the question really shouldn't even be how long ago slavery was, but when did it ever really end. Because the last time that I checked, the 13th Amendment still says slavery is abolished, except for punishment as a crime. Slavery never ended, it only transformed, but I digress until part II.

Myth#7
The Unintelligent Slave

Most times when we read about the enslavement of African people, we automatically associate those who were enslaved, with being dumb. We do this because we have the understanding that slaves in this country, were not taught in most cases how to read or write. As well, if they were caught trying to learn how to read and write, they would be severely beaten or killed. Taking these things into account, many European scholars and historians thought of slaves as dumb people. However, just because most slaves were illiterate, does not mean they weren't intelligent.

Africans even during slavery, were in fact highly intelligent and showed very high abilities to learn at even faster rates than other racial groups in the world. There were many enslaved African people that came up with many of the inventions we still use today. As an old saying has it, the only thing the white men ever invented, was the patent office to steal the black man's inventions. The Patent Act of 1793 and 1836, barred enslaved Africans from obtaining patents because they were not considered citizens. It took until 1861, for Jefferson Davis, president of the confederate States of America, to enact a patent law that would enable Africans to receive protection for their inventions.

Then in 1870, the U.S. government passed a patent law giving all American men, including Africans, the rights to their inventions. However, before the civil war, most inventions by African people could have and in fact were, easily stolen. This was not just predicate to the south, free Africans in the north could not get their invention patented either. One of the most influential inventors in American history, was an African man named Norbert Rillieux.

Norbert Rillieux

Born in 1806 a free man, the son of a mother who was a slave, as well as a father who was a wealthy white engineer. Rillieux, was able to develop a device that heated sugar cane juice in a partial vacuum, reducing its boiling point, allowing much greater efficiency. Subsequently, Rillieux device was developed. Some scholars have called Rillieux's evaporator, the greatest invention in the history of American chemical engineering. Rillieux's evaporator, was adopted in sugar refining.

In addition, it was able to escalate production, reduce the price, and is responsible for transforming sugar into the household item it is today. On the other hand, there were many African slaves who never received any recognition for their inventions. We were always told since a young age, that Eli Whitney invented the cotton gin. However, according to the University of Houston's College of Engineering, Whitney got the idea from a slave known as Sam. Sam's father came up with a kind of comb to get the seeds out of a cotton boll. All Whitney did was mechanize it.

Just ask yourself, why would Eli Whitney invent something to make picking cotton easier and more efficient, when he had slaves to do that? It is amazing when you think about how a man who graduated from Yale, would get his ideas and inventions from slaves who most likely had no form of education at all. The stealing of inventions and credit was not uncommon back then, and there were many more. A slave named Jo Anderson worked closely with Cyrus McCormick, on the development of his famous reaper. You had brothers like Benjamin Banneker, who was born and lived during the time of slavery, yet was the mastermind behind the layout of Washington D.C., reconstructing the bulk of the city's plans, from his presumably photographic memory. Yet Pierre L' Enfant always gets the recognition.

Other names are Benjamin Montgomery, Henry Boyd and Benjamin Bradley. They made inventions but were denied a patent because they were not considered citizens. These were highly intelligent individuals who had many gifts, even though most were never provided with any formal education. African slaves in this country were never dumb or unable learn. They were just never afforded the opportunities to do so.

Another example of our extraordinary gifts mentally that we displayed, was in the medical field. During slavery, it was always well documented and known that the big momma of the plantation took care of everybody; from the newborn babies, to the injured slaves out in the field, to even the same master who accused her of being dumb. Remember slaves were considered nothing but property and in return were treated just like livestock. They rarely, if ever, had any certified medical doctors come give them a checkup. These treatments were only reserved for the master and his family on the plantation.

In fact, in most cases it was up to the big momma of the

plantation to keep everybody healthy and able to work. Many west African slaves brought knowledge of medicine across the Atlantic with them. Along with the indigenous Africans who of course had excellent knowledge of the plants and herbs around them and how they could be used. The health of African people prior to the contact of the Whiteman, was superior to any other place. In parts of Africa and America, you had cases of elders living to be well over a 100.

There was no sickness or serious illnesses in Africa back then, because they used natural herbs and ate right to stay healthy. African slaves in America used these same medical cures as in Africa. Most of the time, the big momma of the plantation would use many of the plants they had growing around the fields, such as snakeroot, may apple, red pepper, boneset, pine needles, comfrey, and red oak to name a few. The big momma of the plantation also understood the various preparations of certain plants that might be considered dangerous. Avoiding the dangerous parts, while extracting and taking advantage of its curative properties. She could use these plants or herbs to cure anything from stomach sickness, to an infection, or even to help a slave heal after a severe lashing.

The Big momma, or the Witch Doctor of the plantation as she was sometimes referred to, had a critical role in everyday plantation life. Who do you think was called when slaves were sick and injured, causing them to be unable to work, in return causing the production of the plantation to drop, thus resulting in a loss of money? Big momma, the medical genius on the plantation, that's who.

Another classic example of this was an enslaved African by the name of Onesimus who lived in Boston in the early 1700's. During a time period in Boston history in which there was a massive outbreak of smallpox plaguing the area. It was the medical genius Onesimus who told Cotton Mather about inoculation. A medical practice or vaccination making one immune to smallpox. A practice that Onesimus claimed had been around for hundreds of years in Africa.

All in all, as you can see, just because slaves had no formal education, doesn't mean they weren't highly intelligent. They were able to come up with some of the best designs, inventions, and natural cures the world has ever seen. All the while trying to survive. However, when they were given a chance, they delivered, doing something no other race had ever done before. According to the National Center for Education Statistics in 1870, about only 20 percent of the slave population was literate. By 1900 that number had grown to about 54 percent and by 1920 it had grown to 80 percent.

No other race in history had grown their literacy rate that fast, given the social and economic conditions we were in just two generations before hand. Keep in mind what our ancestors were still dealing with at the time. Heavy amounts of Jim Crowism, especially in the south, as well as segregated and poorly funded schools and yet they still achieved this amazing feat in a matter of two generations. On top of that, with no real push by the government to properly educate or repair African people in America. This goes back to what I was saying earlier.

It wasn't the fact that we were dumb or somehow mentally inferior to whites, we just had never been granted the opportunities. Even so, we still contributed to many inventions and thoughts that shape America today. Whether it be in areas of production, medicine, or even organizing and planning ways to rebel. We have always been the brains of America, since the beginning.

Myth#8
Honest Abe

One of the biggest myths about slavery in today's point in time is the honest Abe myth. The myth that Abraham Lincoln along with some more good white folks, were so tired of slavery, that they fought a war to end it. A myth that many scholars and historians continue to push. Even politicians have used this myth for their own political purpose. United States Senator Mitch McConnell, said when asked about if he supported the idea for reparations for American descendants of slaves, "We dealt with our original sins of slavery by fighting a civil war". However, when you put these arguments into their proper context, you will be able to see that they couldn't be anything further from the truth.

For example, people that tell you that honest Abe went to war to free the slaves are lying. Because the truth is, Abraham Lincoln went to war to keep the union together. We see further proof of this from letters Abraham Lincoln wrote himself, to one Horace Greeley, during the civil war. In a letter dated August 22nd, 1862, Lincoln said to Greeley "My paramount object in this struggle is to save the Union and is not either to save or to destroy slavery. If I could save the Union without freeing any slave I would do it, and if I could save it by freeing all the slaves I would do it; and if I could save it by freeing some and leaving others alone I would also do that. What I do about slavery, and the colored race, I do because I believe it helps to save the Union; and what I forbear, I forbear because I do not believe it would help to save the Union".

So, as you can see it did not make a difference one way or another if slavery continued or not for Abraham Lincoln, as long as the union was saved. Therefore, in order to save the union Lincoln had no choice but to issue the Emancipation Proclamation on January 1st, 1863. A proclamation which declared "that all persons held as slaves" within the rebellious states "are, and henceforward shall be free." Yet, it is important to note that this document was selective and limited in many ways.

For example, all slaves were not to be set free according to the proclamation, because loyal border states where exempt. Meaning states such as Delaware, Maryland, Kentucky, and Missouri could keep their slaves, as long as they stayed loyal to the union, providing these states with a major advantage at the time, due to the fact that according to the 1860 census, Maryland had over 87,000 slaves, Missouri had over 114,000 slaves and Kentucky had over 225,000 slaves. The state of Delaware was the only bordering state where slavery did not play a major role, due to the fact that they only had 1,798 slaves at the time. The truth is the Emancipation Proclamation, didn't help to free any of our ancestors, it only enabled our ancestors to help free themselves. The reason why I say this, is because a major part of the Proclamation that many historians leave out, is the announced acceptance of black men into the Union Army and Navy.

This is the most important part of the Emancipation Proclamation, because without the participation of black soldiers in the Civil War, the Union might have very well lost the war. Remember during the first 2 years of the civil war, neither side had really gained an advantage with thousands of lives being lost on both sides. The battle of Antietam exemplified that perfectly, where on September 17th, 1862 in Sharpsburg Maryland, more than 22,000 men either lost their lives, were wounded or went missing, making this the bloodiest day in United states military history. Abraham

Lincoln knew he could not continue down this path. After all, the war had resulted in a tactical draw for the union along with 12,410 casualties on their side. It was because of this battle and the number of lives lost, that five days later Lincoln signed the Emancipation Proclamation, in order to finally allow Black soldiers to join the war and fight for their freedom, which became a major turning point in the war.

From the time the Emancipation Proclamation was put into effect, to the end of the civil war, almost 200,000 black soldiers participated. As a group laying to rest any doubts that black troops could or would fight. Helping to win battles and secure key victories like in Vicksburg, Milliken's Bend, Port Hudson and more. The courage and bravery of Black soldiers during the war became stuff of legend. Soldiers such as Robert Smalls, escaped from slavery by stealing a confederate slave ship and sailing north into Union waters.

Robert Smalls

Giving the Union navy a new ship, artillery, ammunition, and key intelligence information from Robert Smalls himself about the confederate army's plans and positions. Soldiers such as Andre Cailloux, who fought to the death in the Siege of Port Hudson. Soldiers like Christian Fleetwood and Aaron Anderson, who received America's highest military decoration, the Medal of Honor, for their actions in the Battle of Chaffin's Farm and on the Potomac river. Yet despite our ancestor's heroic efforts, they were never given the proper compensation, credit and respect they deserved, for saving the union. Instead, they continued to receive the same treatment after the war, as they did before.

Instead, it was Union soldiers who set up concentration camps for free blacks in Natchez Mississippi, after the civil war. Concentration camps with conditions so bad, they would later become known as the Devil's Punch Bowl, where black men, women and children were forced to work against their will. Instead it was Honest Abe himself who suggested that the same black soldiers and people who had just helped him to save the union, should leave the country. That's right, it was Abraham Lincoln who was making plans with congress to send the newly freed slaves to south and central America and then colonize them there. The great ancestor Fredrick Douglass said it best when speaking about Abraham Lincoln. Douglass said, "the President of the United States has become an itinerant colonization preacher, who has made himself look ridiculous by pitching this idea that we should leave the nation of our birth."

Conclusion

During this chapter we have discussed and debunked some of the biggest myths about our ancestors during slavery, and now that we know the truth, it's important that we never forget. See, a lot of people around the country, both black and white, claim that they are tired of hearing and talking about slavery. Which is exactly why, as an American descendant of slaves, we must never get tired of talking about slavery. Every time we do, we are giving a pass to descendants of white Americans who are still benefiting from the fruits of our ancestor's labor. While we, as American descendants of slaves, have received nothing.

No financial compensation, nor mental repair from the atrocities we have suffered from since the beginning. Thus, every time you get a chance, you remind them of what they did and how they are still benefiting from it. Most importantly, remind yourself, so you won't get pulled away from reality and start believing the lies. We must continue to fight for justice, for one of the biggest human atrocities known to man, that no country has yet to be held accountable for; no matter who it makes angry or uncomfortable, because when our ancestors were whipped, bonded, raped, killed and bred like cattle, I'm sure they were angry and uncomfortable too; which is why it's our duty as American descendants of slaves, to fight for justice in the name of our ancestors. Understanding that we have no friends or saviors, we have to save ourselves and that can only come from exposing the lies and revealing the truth.

PART. 2

THE 13TH

"THEY SAID WE CAN'T END SLAVERY TOO
MANY RESIDUALS, SO THEY DON'T CALL
YOU SLAVES NO MORE THEY CALL YOU
CRIMINALS"

-MYSONNE

So often today we love to distance ourselves from our ugly past time. People love to ask questions like "if slavery ended over 100 years ago, there's no excuse for the black man and woman to be struggling"? And to those people I say, you my friend, must not know your history. Not only do you not know your history, but you must not know how to read as well. I say this because to this day, the Constitution clearly states "Neither slavery nor involuntary servitude except as a punishment for a crime whereof the party should have been duly convicted, shall exist within the United States, or any place subject to their jurisdiction". As a result, the practice of slavery never ended, it only transformed and changed names.

Yet according to many white historians and Fox News anchors, it doesn't exist anymore, even though their constitution still says it does. Well, I'm here to officially tell and remind you that the United States of America never ended slavery, and it continues its billion-dollar enterprise in which it built this country to this day. Now we discussed in Part One, the horror of living during the old slavery and what our ancestors dealt with on a regular basis. In this chapter, we will break down and bring to light the knowledge of the new slavery, that the United States created through the 13th Amendment, as well as shine a light on the tactics and codes they use, to keep black people in a marginalized, oppressed and slave like position in the 21st century.

Black Codes

To understand the new slavery, we must first start at the beginning. On April 9, 1865, General Robert E. Lee, surrendered to the Union's Ulysses S. Grant at Appomattox Court House in Virginia, marking the end of the four-year-long Civil War between the North and the South. As a result, later that year on December 6th, 1865, the 13th Amendment was passed and put into law. The 13th Amendment was signed and put into place by Abraham Lincoln. A man who many of our history books today credit with being the person responsible for successfully ending slavery as I mentioned in Part One.

Well the truth is the United States never ended slavery, they only transformed it. As I said before we must understand Lincoln had a singular goal he was trying to accomplish, of reuniting the Union. As a result, slavery would have to come to an end, because that's how the south had grown so powerful in the first place. Remember slavery was not only a huge part of the economy for the south, but it was just as important for states in the north, because seemingly all their products were being produced from slave labor in the south. White America would have to give up slavery, the number one money making tool in America.

This was a major problem and unacceptable in the eyes of white Americans, who deem their whole livelihood on the dependence of free black labor. Therefore, as a solution to the problem, Lincoln and the United States government on December 6th, 1865, came up with the 13th Amendment, basically stating that slavery is abolished except as punishment for a crime. Now giving white Americans a reason to justify the enslavement of African people in America. However, that wasn't good enough. I mean who said that African people would commit crimes now that they were free? Creating once again, another huge problem for the United States.

A country that was built on the enslavement of African people. A country in that 1865, could not stand to see millions of Africans roaming around free under the 13th Amendment. This caused white Americans to systematically force the issue and create what the 13th Amendment would call criminals. Doing so by implementing what are known today as Black Codes and Vagrancy Laws. Black Codes were laws passed by States mainly in the south, but not just exclusively to the south, post-civil war.

These laws had the intent and the effect, of restricting African people's freedom and of compelling them to work in a labor economy, based on low wages or debt. These Black Codes were a counterattack against the millions of an emancipated African. The defining feature of the Black Codes were broad vagrancy tactics, which allow local authorities to arrest Africans for minor infractions and commit them to involuntary servitude. States such as South

Carolina's Black Codes, only apply to persons of color which they classified as anyone having more than one eighth Negro blood. South Carolina had labor contracts especially for black servants who agreed to work for white masters. The contract included that the black servants had to reside on the employer's property, remain quiet, orderly, work from sunup to sunset except on Sundays and not leave the premises or receive visitors without the master's permission.

Masters could also whip servants under the age of 18 to discipline them. Whipping older servants required a judge's approval. Any time lost due to illness would be deducted from service. Servants who quit before the end date of the labor period, could lose all wages and could be arrested and returned to their masters buy a judge. I remind you that this is after the Thirteenth Amendment had been passed. A time when there is supposed to be no more slavery in the United States.

Now I don't know about you, but that sounds like slavery to me. Mississippi for example, was one of the first states to have Black Codes. Mississippi's Black Codes went so far as to making it illegal for blacks to be unemployed. Yes, that's right unemployed. These vagrancy laws allowed the blacks only to rent land within the city limits, effectively preventing African people from earning any income or way of living, through independent farming. If they were caught in violation of these laws, they could be punished by prison time.

These policies and laws that were held in several states such as South Carolina, Mississippi, Florida, Maryland, Louisiana, etc., essentially gave birth to the convict leasing system. A convict leasing system, that did exactly what the 13th Amendment designed it to do, which was to transition the slave plantation from an individual owned commodity, to a state-owned commodity and resource. Doing so by providing labor to private parties, such as plantation owners and corporations like, The Tennessee Coal and Iron Company. For example, according to Cyndi Banks, convict leasing was huge business in some states like Alabama, where in 1898, some 73% of Alabama's entire annual state revenue came from convict leasing.

Guards watching a convict-lease work gang in Birmingham.

Georgia was another state who relied heavily on the convict leasing programs. Provisional Governor Thomas Ruger awarded the first convict lease to William A. Fort of the Georgia and Alabama railroads, on May 11th, 1868. Fort was given 100 African prison labors for one year, at the price of 2,500 dollars. Out of the 100, 16 of the prisoners died during that first year due to the harsh work conditions. Within 5 years, convict leasing was a major source of revenue for the state of Georgia. Over a span of 18 months from 1872 to 1873, the hiring out of prison labor brought the state of Georgia more than 35,000 dollars.

This led to a law being passed in 1876, that endorsed the leasing of State prisoners to one or more companies for at least 20 years. Keep in mind, most of these men serving extreme time were doing time for petty offenses, due to Black Codes and laws. George W. Cable, author of "The Grandsires" wrote in a paper on " The convict lease system" before a prison congress in Kentucky. "In the Georgia penitentiary in 1880, a total of nearly 1200 prisoners, only 76 were serving as low a term as one year. Only 52 others as low as 2 years. Only 76 of this as low a term of 3 years. While those who were under the sentence of 10 years and over was 538, although 10 years as the rolls show, is the utmost length of time that a convict can be expected to remain alive in a Georgia penitentiary. Six men were under sentence for simple assault and battery-mere fisticuffing- One of 2 years, two of 5 years, one of 6 years and 7 years and one of 8.

In other words, a large majority of these men had been arrested for simply stealing without breaking in or violence. As a result, they were virtually condemned to be worked and mistreated to death. One man was under a 20-year sentence for stealing a hog. 12 men were sentenced to the South Carolina Penitentiary on no other findings but misdemeanor, commonly atoned for by a fine of a few dollars, in which thousands of the state inhabitants being white, are constantly committing with impunity". Mr Cables goes on to say in his paper, "The Georgia Convict Leasing System was as cruel as all the other southern states. Of the 215 prisoners in Georgia serving sentences of more than 10 years, only 15 were white".

A Georgia chain gang builds a road in Oglethorpe county in 1941

African men, women, and children were herded together like cattle, chained down and forced to work like their descendants that came before them. It's important for us to know this, so we can bring it full circle in order to see the big picture. First, in 1865 the 13th Amendment was put into place, making millions of formerly enslaved Africans free. However, only to a certain degree. This is where the Black Codes come in, making it illegal for African people in some states, to be homeless, unemployed, or to be in large groups after dark. Not to mention providing severe and harsh sentencing when accused and convicted of a crime.

Sentencing that led to them being put into convict leasing programs in which they were sold to companies, private corporations, and in some cases plantation owners for work, forming nothing but the new era of slavery. It was a sort of evil genius in a way, that white society had found a loophole in putting African people right back into chains, while at the same time saving face from religious beliefs and persecution, by simply saying these people deserve to be slaves because they're "criminals". An excuse many whites still use to justify the mistreatment of African people. Yet when you dig a little deeper, you find out that they had brothers serving 8 years and forcing them to work because they got into a fist fight, or serving time for being homeless or serving a 20 year sentence for stealing a damn hog, as George W. Cable wrote in his paper to Kentucky congress. Keep in mind the reason why we had to steal or commit crimes in the first place.

We had to steal because for the last 250 plus years, we had been locked up and enslaved like animals. We had not been allowed to buy land, acquire assets or start our own businesses. We were not allowed to have anything, not even our intellectual property, which was stolen from us. In most cases, we never saw a dime or a dollar for our labor. Therefore, upon release from bondage at the end of the Civil War, we had nothing to speak of.

Most, if not all slaves, were in violation of one or more Black Codes from the jump, not to mention the federal government went out of its way, to deny any sort of reparations or restitution to the now millions of formerly enslaved African people. Even denying what many leaders under William T Sherman's special field order number 15 had promised, which was 40 acres and a mule for hundreds of years of unpaid labor.

40 Acres and a Mule

William T Sherman's special field order number 15, could have changed the course of history for African people in this country, due to the language of the contract. Section 1 States " the islands of Charleston, south, the abandoned rice fields along the river for 30 miles back from the sea, and the country bordering the St. Johns River in Florida, are reserved and set apart for the settlement of the Negroes now made free by the act of war and the proclamation of the President of the United States". It then goes on to state in section two "...on the Islands, and in settlements hereafter to be established, no white person whatever, unless military officers and soldiers' detailed for duty, will be permitted to reside; and the exclusive management of affairs will be left to the free people themselves, by the laws of war and orders of the President of the United States, the Negro is free, and must be dealt with as such". To even sit back and process that in 2019 is mind boggling.

Can you imagine African people being given their own land to start farming, business, and for creating an economic foundation, at the same time, not having to worry about the people who have spent the last hundreds of years trying to oppress us? The reason why we wouldn't have to worry, is because section three specified "each family should have a plot of no more than 40 acres of tillable ground and when it borders on some water channel, with not more than 800 feet of waterfront, in the possession of which land the military authorities will afford them protection until such time as they can protect themselves or until congress shall regulate their title". Having this land and opportunity for African people for our years of suffering could have possibly changed the African experience in America as we know it. Unfortunately, our hopes and dreams were crushed swiftly and bluntly. Because just for a split-second, African people had forgotten where they were and who they were dealing with. We were in the land of thieves and the home of the Klan.

Just as African people saw how powerful William T Sherman's special field order number 15 was, so did our oppressors, America's white body government. The institution that was founded and rose to power from the labor of our African ancestors. Therefore, in the fall of 1865 Andrew Johnson who was a democrat, Lincoln's successor and sympathizer with the south, overturned the Order and as Barton Meyer sadly concludes, "returned the land along the South Carolina, Georgia and Florida coast, to the Planters who had originally owned". The same plantation owners I might add, who acquired so much land and capital, because of the enslavement of African people. The same plantation owners, who 4 years earlier picked up a gun and declared war on the United States of America, instead of giving it to the formerly enslaved Africans, who fought side-by-side with the north to help win the war and keep the union.

Isn't this white supremacy one-on-one for you? Instead of having a foundation on which to build upon, the African Freemen were left penniless, uneducated, homeless and friendless in the hostile south. Without land reparations or tools, they had little choice but offer the market their only resource, which was themselves in the physical form. As an available trained cheap labor force blacks stepped into a predictable future of sharecropping to make a living. Like the ones in South Carolina, where you could be whipped, and work from sunup to sundown. Meaning life after the 13th Amendment for African people hadn't changed.

Only now, as an African person in America, you supposedly had a choice, which in most cases ended up as the same result. Work for a white Master sharecropping, getting paid barely enough to survive while working in slave-like conditions. Or on the other side, you can refuse to go back to the plantation to work, which would cause a violation and put you in a convict leasing program where they forced you to work. These were the two choices for African men and women post-Civil War, some freedom huh?

Origins of Policing

It is a sad but common story to turn on the TV in our house and see yet another black king and queen shot and killed by the police. It is a theme that many of us African people almost have become accustomed to living in America. It makes many of us beg the question why? Why is it that we are always being gunned down like animals and then as the victims, being treated worse than the perpetrators who carried out the crime? No matter the situation, we can be unarmed like our brother Michael Brown was, only for them to come out and tell us "oh well he should have never been fighting the cop". We can just be at the corner of the street making a hustle like our brother Eric Gardner was, when he was choked out.

Eric Gardner being put in Choke hold by Daniel Pantaleo

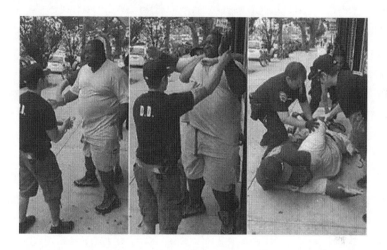

Only for them to say, "oh well he should have never been resisting". Acting as if when someone jumps on your neck and starts choking you, you're going to be calm. We can be riding home from work with our family after a long day, and get pulled over by the cops for driving while black; yet out of respect, let them know we have a gun in the car, so the police won't feel surprised or threatened by the situation. Only to have our act of good faith backfire on us, and have four bullets unloaded in our chest, like our brother Philando Castile had. As a matter of fact, we can even be sitting at home eating a bowl of ice cream minding our own business, only to have an off-duty cop kick in our door and blow our brains out like our brother Botham Jean; which leaves many of us as African people around the country lost and confused.

Confused from the fact that the very police departments that we pay through our tax dollars to serve and protect us, constantly and on a regular basis, continue to execute us. Why is the system of policing in America so broken? The answer is simple, it is not broken. It's being run and executed the exact way it is supposed to, protecting and serving the people of the United States from its 40 + million free slaves, controlling and returning them to their rightful place, prison AKA, the new plantation. But if they cannot be returned at a fast-enough rate, execution will also do.

The birth of policing in this country, has a long legal and political history. A history that has shown us that policing in this country, has always been based off the beliefs and conditions of that time. Which is why the institution of slavery and the control of blacks according to many scholars and historians, were the two most formidable historic features of shaping early policing tactics. Therefore, slave patrols and night watches became modern-day police departments as we know them today. Many police departments around the country, especially in the south, began as slave patrols.

The first form of slave patrols was created in the Carolina colonies. Now not only did the slave patrols operate through country law, but they made it mandatory for white males to be a part of the slave patrol unit. In essence, controlling African people was a group effort. Slave patrol units were often called patrollers, paddy rollers and paddies just to name a few. Some of that same terminology still applies today.

You will hear officers use the term, we put the suspect in the back of the "Patty wagon". This is nothing but old slave terminology that is still used from back in the day. When you look at these slave patrols, they had three primary responsibilities. First was to chase down, handover and return slaves to their owners. The second function was to provide a form of organized terror, to deter slaves from starting revolts or revolutions. Third or finally, was to maintain a form of discipline for slave workers who were subject to similar justice outside of the law, if they violated any plantation rules.

They also had little tasks, like to go from plantation to plantation, to make sure no slave was wondering around or walking without a pass. However, most times pass or no pass, they would still beat or even kill the slave for intimidation purposes, to send a message. These tasks were started by local government and even improved by Congress, to help slave patrols carry out their duty effectively. In Georgia for example, a generation before the American Revolution laws were passed in 1755 and 1757, that required all plantation owners, or their male white employees, to be members of the Georgia Military, and for those armed militia members, to make monthly inspections of the quarters of all slaves in the state. Dr. Carl T Bogus, wrote for the University of California Law Review in 1998, "Georgia statutes require patrols under the direction of Commissioners Militia Officers, to examine every Plantation each month and authorize them to search all Negro houses for offensive weapons and ammunition and to apprehend and give 20 lashes to any slave found outside Plantation grounds".

In fact to dive even deeper from a national level of policing, the real reason the 2nd Amendment was ratified and why it says "state" instead of "country", was to preserve the slave patrol militias in the southern states that had an effect on the nationwide economy, which was also necessary to get Virginia's vote. One of the founders of the Second

Amendment argued that "southerners' property (slaves), would be lost under the new constitution and the resulting slave uprising would be less than peaceful or tranquil". Henry then said to Madison, "I see a great deal of property of the people of Virginia in jeopardy and their peace and tranquility gone". It was only then that Madison, who had already begun to prepare and propose amendments to the Constitution, changed his first draft of one that addressed the militia issue, to make sure it was unambitious, that the southern states can maintain their slave patrol militias. Madison's first draft of the Second Amendment originally said, "The right of the people to keep and bear arms shall not be infringed, a well-armed and a well-regulated militia being the best security of a free country; but no person religiously scrupulous of bearing arms shall be compelled to render military service in person".

Patrick Henry, James Madison, as well as others however, wanted southern states to preserve the slave patrol militias independent of the federal government. So, this is why Madison changed the word from country to state and redrafted the Second Amendment to how we see it today. Now when you take into consideration the history behind the Second Amendment, we can now have some understanding of how in 2020, we still look and are treated like slaves of the 1800's. A perfect example of this is the shooting death of our brother Philando Castile.

Philando Castile

A brother who was a role model and a respected leader in his community, who helped and taught many children in his community how to grow up and be responsible human beings. Now how is it that Philando Castile, an African American, who was a law-abiding citizen his whole life, had been pulled over more than 49 times prior to his death? Yes, that number is correct. 49 times in a span of 13 years, Philando Castile was pulled over; often for minor infractions. We're talking about being pulled over for turning into a parking lot without signaling, failing to repair a broken seat belt, and driving at night with an unlit license plate. These are just some of the infractions our brother Philando Castile was charged with.

Now these infractions that he was pulled over for are nothing but in the new age of Black Codes. Philando Castile was being harassed and stalked by the cops, not because of his driving, but because as Miss Valerie Castile said, "her son was driving while black". Therefore, all these instances of "driving while black", finally came to a head on July 6, 2016;

when police officer Jeronimo Yanez, pulled over Mr. Castile yet again, allegedly for a cracked taillight. After following the initial instructions of the officer, Jeronimo Yanez asked for Mr. Castile's license and registration. Being the Law-abiding citizen Mr. Castile was, he made sure to make the officer aware before reaching for his license, that he does have a gun in the car.

This is something our brother did not have to do or tell the officer, according to the law. Unfortunately, this act of good faith caused Officer Yanez to panic and start to shout, "don't pull it out" which in the video Mr. Castile clearly says, "I'm not". Yanez still proceeded to panic and unload four shots into a car with our brother's queen in the passenger seat, as well as a child in the back. Why is this? Why did a simple act of good faith cause our brother to lose his life in a matter of seconds?

The reason why, is because of the origins of what policing was founded on, which still holds true to this day, which is they are nothing but modern-day slave patrols, carrying out the same duties they had since the first one was founded in 1704. To instill fear and discipline into the black population. Understand, when they pulled Mr. Castile over in Falcon Heights Minnesota, which is a predominantly white neighborhood, they weren't wondering about his taillight, they were wondering what this slave is doing out here and where is his pass. The same thing they were wondering the previous 49 times. Then once they had stopped him, pulled him over and found out he had a gun, just like back during slavery, it didn't matter if he had a pass or not. In the police eyes he was an armed slave and a threat to society as we know it. This is how the system was and how it still is today. Don't believe me?

A prime example is when the Philando Castile case reached a verdict. There was outrage across the country from all races and groups of people. Yet strangely enough you noticed there was one group who stayed quiet. A group that many would expect to be the loudest and the most vocal about the case. The National Rifle Association, or as we know them today as the NRA.

The NRA is supposed to be a nonprofit organization, which advocates for gun rights granted to American citizens. The organization has been quick to defend other gun owners who made national news in the past. Yet, it seemed on this case, when dealing with Mr. Castile, an African man who has a valid permit to carry, the cat had their tongue. The NRA was silent because they know this is what the 2nd Amendment was meant for, to allow the slave patrol to control the slaves. Nothing more and nothing less.

When the constitution says you have the right to bear arms, they were never talking about us as African people. It was referring to the slave patrols and the members of the white society. Therefore, we must stop settling for the same tired ass excuse "this was an isolated incident," or "all cops aren't bad". These are nothing more than excuses. It does not matter if all cops are not bad. The problem is the system, that allows the bad cops to make a living terrorizing our communities.

This is unacceptable, it's like our brother Colin Kaepernick said, "A system that perpetually condones the killing of people without consequences, doesn't need to be revisited, it needs to be dismantled". You see these race soldiers, that continue to go out there and carry out these senseless murders, are just the puppets. Our goal needs to be to take down and punish whoever is pulling the strings. Remember we are at war with a system, not individuals. We must also stay woke to the fact that after these officers' murder someone, they are getting paid leave, and being sheltered and walk through the process as if they are the victim. Walking liars like Darren Wilson, who sat on a stand and said that the 6 foot 4, 200 plus pound Michael Brown, punched him twice in the face with full force. He even went so far as to describe our brother Michael Brown as the Hulk. Yet when pictures were revealed on Darren Wilson shortly after the incident, he did not have a scratch or bruise on his face.

The face of Darren Wilson after altercation with Michael Brown

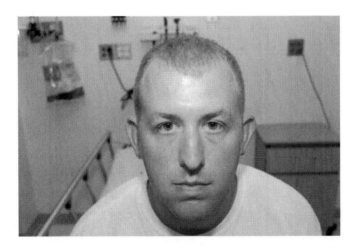

As a matter of fact, it was barely red, which is important to note because he's white, and we all know that if white folks stand out in the sun for 30 minutes, their face would be redder than Darren Wilson's was in this picture. But they told us, the public, to believe Darren Wilson was punched twice by the Incredible Hulk, and the hulk left no marks or bruises to speak of. Yet with all of these weird accusations made in Darren Wilson's story, he was not cross-examined once. The prosecutor never questioned Darren Wilson on his side of the story. The prosecutor even went so far as to guide him along like a baby. Asking him questions designed to help Darren Wilson meet the conditions of a self-defense plea.

On the flip side the prosecution went out of its way to paint every witness that supported Michael Brown's side of the story, as an unreliable and lying witness. All in all, leading to the acquittal of Darren Wilson. Which is why I always say it's a system that we are at war with. Not one bad cop, or judge, or prosecutor. Our goal is to bring the whole system down, in which we were and still are enslaved under.

The fact is, when you look at the history in this country of policing in America, you will discover that it is an ugly one. Tactics first used by the slave patrols in the south, still apply to modern-day policing, along with their racist policies and ideologies. Slave patrol, the Klu Klux Klan as well as other Neo-Nazi and white supremacists, are still alive and well. The only difference is these extremist groups just traded in their traditional attire for a police uniform. We saw proof of this in 2006, when the FBI released an extensive report raising the alarm of white supremacist groups, who were "historically interested in infiltration into law enforcement communities or recruiting law enforcement personnel".

In Los Angeles for example, a US District Court Judge found in 1991, that members of a local sheriff's department, had formed a Neo-Nazi gang that had habitually terrorized the black community. John Burge, a police detective and rumored KKK member, was fired and eventually prosecuted in 2008, on charges relating to the torture of at least one hundred and twenty black men during his decade-long career. Burge notoriously referred to an electronic shock device he used during interrogation, as the "nigger box". Also, Cleveland officials found that a number of police officers had scrawled "racist or neo Nazi graffiti throughout their Department locker rooms. In Texas, two police officers were fired when it was discovered they were Clansman. One of them said he had tried to boost membership by giving an application to fellow officers he thought shared "white, Christian, Heterosexual values".

Yet even with the FBI's current knowledge of the situation. The FBI has not publicly addressed the situation or made a serious plan of action since 2006. Only acknowledging the problem that has never been a secret to the black community. Only an issue the dominant society has not been willing to address. People such as former FBI director James Comey, as well in reports done by US Department of Homeland Security, all have acknowledged white supremacist groups in law enforcement.

Not to mention the resurgence of the right-wing extremist groups in the last decades. Groups that capitalized on the election of Barack Obama; using the election to focus their efforts on recruiting new members, mobilizing existing supporters and broadening their agenda through propaganda, specifically stating after Obama's election, extremist groups have targeted ex-military veterans to exploit their skills in military knowledge. However, as usual, when faced with mounting criticism, Terry Janet Napolitano disavowed the document and apologized to the veteran community. Another example of white supremacy one-on-one. Instead of apologizing to the victims, Black people in America, you deflect and apologize to the veterans, allowing white supremacists to continue to infiltrate law enforcement, like Bart Alsbrook, Robert Stamm, Charles Anderson and more did.

These are the tactics and strategies that we discussed in Part 3 volume I of Voice of the Ancestors, when we talked about the religion of white supremacy. But getting back to the point, last but not least, I must highlight one more thing that we should be aware of in the system of policing in

America. The physical value they put on the African. So many times, we in the African Community have become accustomed to receiving no justice. Then a couple months later, receiving civil suit money. Most times for wrongful death.

Philando Castile's family for example, received no justice for the murder of their loved one. Yet they received a 3-million-dollar settlement. Trayvon Martin's family received no justice for their loved one yet received a 1-million-dollar settlement. Eric Garner's family received no justice for their loved one yet received a 5.9-million-dollar settlement. This list goes on and on and on. According to the Huffington Post, more than a billion dollars has been awarded to victims' families in settlements over the last 10 years. Proving the model in America is that we will pay you for your love one's death but will not give you justice.

Bringing us to the conclusion as D.L. Hughley puts it, "not only is justice blind but she is a banker". This is why we have to watch these lawyers, black or white, who go into these cases looking strictly for settlement money. This is not progress, and it undermines us as a community when we fight for justice, allowing our oppressors to think they can pay their way out of a crime. See, notice how once these families receive their settlement money, in most cases they stay very quiet and you never hear from them again. The reason being because it's shut up or guilt money for a crime the local law enforcement said was never committed in the first place.

America tells us no crime was committed, but then pays us millions of dollars for a wrongful death. Don't you find that strange? We look at a million dollars in the African community, as if it's a lot of money, allowing them to give us 5 or 6 million dollars in exchange for a not guilty verdict. Let me be clear, no amount of money could ever bring back our murdered brothers and sisters lost to the system. However, when you have lawsuit settlements like Erin Andrews, who received 55 million dollars because a stalker recorded a video of her. Or you have the real Hulk Hogan, not our brother Michael Brown who Darren Wilson accused, to be getting 31 million dollars in a privacy lawsuit for a sex tape.

This is proof we have a serious problem; especially, when you compare these settlements to the $1.9 million settlement for Sandra Bland, $6.5 million settlement for Walter Scott, and the $1.5 million settlement for Michael Brown. These settlement numbers are a spit in the face of all African people worldwide. That a white man and woman's sex tape are worth five to six times more than an African life. However, remember this is how the system was designed to work, because to them you were and still are, three fifths of a human being. To them you're still a slave.

Propaganda Campaign

As we have talked about in previous Parts, the very foundation of America was built on the enslavement of African people. African people who were responsible for building the railroads, cities, schools and stabilizing the economy as a whole. Fast-forwarding all the way up until today, not very much has changed. A heavy part of America's original core values still remains in tack. One being, keeping the native African population controlled and enslaved. Only now in 2019, it is done in a much different style and manner than in times of slavery.

Today's white supremacist agendas are pasted through propaganda and smoke screen tactics. In 2019 there is no better way to do this than through our modern-day prison system in America, which is kept full through the propaganda our media and politicians push. An argument that is strongly supported by the evidence below, beginning with a simple fact. The United States, the so-called land of the free and the home of the brave, has a population of over 300 million people. Meaning the United States only makes up about 4.4% of the world's total population. However, the United States makes up almost a quarter of the world's prison population, ranging anywhere from 22 to 25 percent, making the world's highest prison population, right here in the United States.

1 out of every 4 prisoners is locked up in America

Research therefore concludes that 716 people per hundred thousand, are in prison in the United States. A rate that might not seem high, but compared to the rest of the world, is. The United States Prison rate is about 6 times Canada's rate, between 6 to 9 times Western European countries rate and between 2 to 10 times northern European countries rate. Another interesting theme to point out as well is that the United States prison rates are much higher than underdeveloped countries. African countries that they portray through media as savage and run down, all have a lower prison rate.

For example, the likes of Kenya, Nigeria, and South Africa, all places Donald Trump referred to as "shit hole countries" all have a lower prison rate. Due to the simple fact that one out of four prisoners locked up around the world, are locked up in the United States. The place whose motto is, the land of the free and the home of the brave. If this is true, the question must be free for who? Anyone who is a non-black that's who.

According to a study done in 2014 by the NAACP, black people in America constituted 2.3 million of the 6.8 million correctional population. That's about 34% of the total prison population. When you compare that to the fact that black people only make up 14% of the total population in the United States, these are alarming numbers. These numbers however are no surprise when we look at the 13th Amendment that still says slavery is abolished, except as punishment for a crime. From slavery, to the convict leasing system, to modern day prisons.

The facts are a nice chunk of the African population is still enslaved physically, just like their ancestors were. Therefore, if you haven't received a proper wakeup call by now, welcome to the new slavery, where African people are incarcerated at more than five times the rate of whites. Welcome to the new slavery, where the imprisonment rate of African women is twice that of white women. Welcome to the new slavery, where nationwide, African children represent 32% of the children who are arrested, 42% of the children who are detained and 52% of the children whose cases are judicially waived to Criminal Court. Welcome to the new slavery, welcome the new plantation.

Can you see the picture now, is it clear to you? As I told you before, the United States did not destroy slavery, it just transformed it. The new goal is mass incarceration, to put

Africans back on the plantation and working for cheap or free. Political leaders will tell you it's not a racial thing, it's about keeping the community safe. This is true, according to a 2014 study by the US Department of Justice that states, a majority of blacks in jail or in prison, are in for violent offenses. Yet when it comes to the position of how those offenses came about, white America turns a blind eye, refuses to accept their share of responsibility, but have no problem blaming us.

Whenever African people speak up against the system of injustice in the United States, whether it be against police brutality or mass incarceration, it always seems to bring about white America's most famous quote as it pertains to African people "what about black on black crime". A quote that has produced big business for the dominant white society, by creating a narrative that these negroes are so dangerous, that they need to be locked up in order to prevent them from hurting other people and themselves. A common narrative in white media outlets around the country. We can come out and say we are marching to end police brutality in America. The response by white America and the dominant society will be, "what about black on black crime". If we as African people want to discuss the inequalities in education and unemployment, the response is, "what about black on black crime".

The answer to all of the white people who love to holler this phrase, what about black on black crime every time they are faced with a racial issue that black people bring forth, is simple, "What about it". The truth is there is no such thing as black on black crime. It is just simply a crime. The cornerstone of the argument black on black crime, stems from several FBI reports that shows that about 90% of black people who are murdered, are murdered by other black people. A fact that many activists and leaders in our

Community, have tried to address hands on for years. Many mainstream media outlets choose to ignore these efforts and spew the lie that the only time black people get mad is when they're killed by white police officers or members from other races. Which couldn't be further from the truth. "Stop the Violence" has been a chorus song in the black community for decades, since KRS-1 made "self-destruction" in 1989 or through Hollywood with movies like "Boyz in the Hood".

Album Self Destruction by KRS-one

The chorus "Stop the Violence" has always been on the top of our to-do list as a people. The problem is, just from watching your local news or reading your local newspaper you would think race or race violence only existed in the black community. No, no, no, see what they don't want you to know, is that most white people who are killed, are killed by other white people. Based on the FBI's 2013 uniform crime report, about 83% of white people who are murdered, are murdered by other white people. Yet you never see this as a front-page news story. Why is that?

Because the whole purpose of bringing up black on black crime is to distract you from the issue at hand, no matter what it is. Most people who use this as an excuse, know there's no such thing as black on black crime. It is simply crime. Even in 2012, the FBI released a report saying "from 1993 to 2008 among homicides reported to the FBI for which the victim offender relationship was known, between 21% and 27% of the homicides were committed by strangers and between 73% and 79% were committed by offenders known to the victim". In other words, what the FBI and statistics show, is that people are more likely to commit a crime against the people they live around. These are the facts. Not that African people hate themselves and are born killers or savages as the mainstream media likes to portray, who have no regard for human life.

Black people are more likely to be murdered by other blacks, because that's who most of us live around. White people are more likely to be murdered by other white people, because that's who they mostly live around. Chinese people are more likely to be murdered by other Chinese people, because that's who they mostly live around. Yet they are so focused on black on black crime. I didn't see anybody in the white mainstream media saying anything about "white on white crime" when Adam Lanza went and killed 20 children and 6 adults in the Sandy Hook shooting, or Baldwin James Holmes, when he walked into a crowded theater and opened fire killing 12 people and injuring 70 others.

Nor did you hear the term white on white crime, in countless other mass shootings involving white perpetrators and white victims. Was anybody yelling what about white on white crime then? The reason being is simple, because it was just seen as a crime not a same race killing. Nevertheless, since white people love to focus their attention on black on black crime, we can do that. You see Africans in America, are in a unique situation.

First, we have to take some self-accountability as African people. I'm all for the idea that we have to repair ourselves from the trauma we have suffered from, due to 400 years of oppression. I say this, because it is obvious no other race or structure of government will. We must begin to stop settling for the narrative that we are criminals and thugs by nature and get on code as African people, by determining what actions and behaviors will be acceptable and not acceptable in our community. We must begin to police and structure ourselves, so there will be some accountability put in place in our community. Where I differ, however, from many mainstream media accounts, as well as other politicians and leaders in the community, is I say our oppressors must also be held accountable.

This message here, is for all white people who love to holler "get over it" or what about "black on black crime". When are our oppressors going to take responsibility for their actions and the trauma they have caused for African people? America's race situation is unique, as best-selling author Jay Morrison says "I liken it to someone who has been kidnapped or a woman or child who has been molested and been molested for several years. Then all of a sudden, they're pushed out the house after several years and go out in the streets and act promiscuous. You blame them for being promiscuous, but you never blame the person who caused the trauma".

That is exactly what has happened to African people in America. If white people do want to know why there's so much "black on black crime" in America? Look in the mirror. Do you remember when our white supremacist government filtered African people into ghettos, or have you just forgot? Let's take a minute to refresh white folk's memory.

They filtered us into the ghettos that we still remain in today, through redlining that started in the 1930's after the Home Owners Loan Corporation was created by Franklin Roosevelt's Administration. Redlining is a discriminatory pattern of disinvestments and obstructive lending practices that act as an impediment to home ownership among Africans in America. As a consequence of redlining, neighborhoods that local banks saw as unfit for investment, were left underdeveloped or in despair. For example, in 1988, a series of Pulitzer prize-winning articles were written under the title "The Color of Money".

The Color of Money a series of articles on lenders avoiding middle-income black neighborhoods

In the articles Atlanta Journal Constitution reporter Bill Dedman, described how Atlanta Banks still discriminated by the racial designation of neighborhoods. Dedman illustrated how these banks were nearly twice as likely to lend to homeowners and perspective home buyers in low-income white neighborhood as in affluent black areas. Attempts to improve these neighborhoods by the black community were then denied and labeled by financial institutions as too risky or simply rejected outright. When existing businesses collapsed, new ones were not allowed to replace them, often leaving entire black blocks empty and crumbling; even though the African community were frequently limited in their access to capital to start our own banks, grocery stores, retail stores etc. One notable exception to this rule of redlining as it was back then and still is today, was the pro liberation of liquor stores and bars.

Businesses that never seemed to be viewed by the bank as financially risky. The result of redlining also led to an appreciable drop in employment opportunities in these neighborhoods, as perspective small-scale employers where declined to locate there. This is important to note, because any historian or scholar of crime, will tell you when there is a lack of jobs in the community, crime goes up. When there are plenty of jobs, crime goes down. In the case of black communities that were subjugated to redlining, crimes went up, especially in the inner cities.

The crime that followed in the wake of these declining neighborhoods made future investments less likely. From a broader perspective, the high level of crime seemingly justified the initial redlining. So now after years, even decades of redlining, the system of white supremacy was able to implement stage two. In comes the CIA, pushing cocaine into the black community. Across the country in black communities, cocaine was on the streets. Freeway Rick Ross, who most famously created a crack empire in LA during the 1980s, was said to be a key figure in the CIA's operation.

The connection between the CIA and the overflowing drugs in the black community, was brought to light by Pulitzer prize-winning journalist Gary Webb, who stunned the world with his Dark Alliance newspaper series, investigating the connection between the CIA and crack explosion in the predominantly black neighborhood of south Los Angeles. Even before the 1980s, starting in the late 1960s early 1970s, you begin to see drugs overwhelmingly flow into the black communities, with famous drug lords such as Frank Lucas and Nicky Barnes creating monster drug empires, from Harlem all the way to Atlanta. Drugs such as heroin, cocaine and more, were easy and accessible to get, turning what would be normal high school boys, into drug Kingpins, willing to harm and poison their own community to survive. People from the outside looking in, are so quick to judge and blame black people for our situation, like we created it. The government gave black people two choices through redlining.

You're either going to starve or you're going to sell dope. Because remember, we couldn't get bank loans so we could open our own businesses in order to employ members of our community. Nor was the government providing jobs in our neighborhood for our people to work. The American government economically cast us out to fend for ourselves. Forcing many black men and women to turn to the crack rock, not only as a means of putting food on the table, but as an escape. Now again, we find ourselves as members of the African community in a unique situation, in the sense that we are seemingly the victim of governmental experiments. This time using drugs to destroy our neighborhoods.

Yet at the same time, when reflecting on our history in the United States, these experiments are nothing new. From a Government standpoint, it was nothing but business as usual, not only by allowing drugs to come in and be filtered into the African Community, but then turning around and locking us up for it. A prime example of this is the War on Drugs campaign in the 1970's. The term the "War on Drugs" was popularized by the media shortly after then President Richard Nixon's special message to Congress in which he declared drug abuse Public Enemy Number One. "The War on Drugs" were a set of drug policies put in place by President Richard Nixon, that was supposed to discourage the production, distribution and consumption of illegal drugs. However, these new policies at the end of the day, we're set up to control the African population and put us right back on the prison plantation.

Nine years after Nixon coined the expression War on Drugs, statistics showed only a minor increase in the total number imprisoned. Yet after, in the 1980s during the crack epidemic, things began to change. According to Austin McVey in an Article he helped write called, "The 1989 NCCD prison population forecast: the impact of the War on Drugs" he stated in the decade of the 1980's, drug-related offenses rose 126%. In just 18 months from December 1987 to June 1989, the nation's prison population grew by 15.3%. In the first 6 months of 1989, the nation's prison population grew by over 7%, which at the time was an all-time historic increase.

He then goes on to state that, despite the increased use of incarceration, especially for blacks, Hispanics and drug offenders, there has been no positive impact on crime rates. In fact, crime rates have increased by nearly 13% since. The problem then grew increasingly worse in the next decade. From 1990 through 2000 an increasing number of drug offenses accounted for 27% of the total gross number of black inmates. That's more than any other race.

Here are some more interesting facts provided by the NAACP and the Human Rights Watch since the war on drug policies were put into effect. Nationwide, blacks comprise of 62% of drug offenders admitted into the state prison. In seven states blacks constitute between 80 and 90% of all people sent to prison on drug charges. Nationwide, black men are sent to state prison on drug charges at 13 times the rate of white men. 2 out of 5 blacks sent to prison are convicted on drug offenses compared to 1 out every 4 whites. One in every 20 black men over the age of 18 in the United States is in state or federal prison, compared to one in 180 white men.

In the 2015 National Survey on Drug Use and Health, about 17 million whites and 4 million Africans reported having used illicit drugs within the last month. Blacks represent 12.5% of illicit drug users, but 29% of those arrested for drug offenses, and 33% of those incarcerated in State facilities for drug related charges. These are just a few of the many lopsided statistics proving the War on Drugs targeted to set out and destroy black families. Most times in America, we ignore the statistics because they're just numbers on a paper and many eyes. Yet they are far more than that. You can hear and see that for yourself from aids of Richard Nixon.

In 2016 a news report broke that one of Richard Nixon's top advisors and key figures in the Watergate scandal, said the War on Drugs was created as a political tool to fight blacks and hippies. John Ehrlichman, the man responsible for domestic policies under Richard Nixon, stated these comments in a 22-year-old interview with Dan Baum. "The Nixon campaign in 1968 and the Nixon white house after that, had two enemies: the anti-war left, and black people".

He went on to say "you understand what I'm saying? We knew we couldn't make it illegal to be either against the war or blacks, but by getting the public to associate hippies with marijuana and blacks with heroin and then criminalizing both heavily, we could disrupt those communities. We could arrest their leaders, raid their homes, break up their meetings, and vilify them night after night on the evening news. Did we know we were lying about the drugs? Of course, we did".

Now this is coming from the perpetrators themselves. It was nothing but a cover-up for the real war, which was war on black people. As I said in Voice of the Ancestors Volume I and I'll say again. The number one rule of white supremacy is deception. Only when we expose their deceptive ways is when we will see them for what they are.

Prison for Profit

One thing we as Black people must learn, is that there are levels to our oppression, along with many layers that help to keep us bottled down and held back. During this part I touched on the early years of the convict leasing system, especially during the reconstruction era. The reason I did so, was to help you understand that the very foundation of the prison system in 2019, is still built under those same principles. However, in today's age unlike during reconstruction, there is a twist. This twist comes in the form of privatization on the new plantation.

During the reconstruction era, prison systems belong to the states. A trend that would hold true for a century, plus it was only then, in the late 1970's and early 1980's, that the government decided to truly give the power back to the people. Before this time period private prisons didn't exist. Interesting timing, because it was around the same time the CIA dropped the drugs off, and Nixon started the whole

War on Drugs campaign. Remember though, initially during the first 9 years after Nixon coined the term War on Drugs, statistics only showed a minor increase in the total number imprisoned.

It wasn't until the 1980's under President Reagan, when incarceration reached soaring heights. Which in the end, results increased the demand for the development of privatization. There are many reasons why the privatization prison systems are still in high demand today. For one thing, the prison system has gradually become more privatized, to the extent that the state has shifted some responsibilities for housing prisoners from the public to the private sector, sometimes as a deliberate economic revitalization. Revitalization strategy, meaning a market strategy to use when the product reaches the maturity stage of a product's life cycle, and profits have drastically fallen.

In an attempt to bring the product (prisoners) back in the market and secure the source of equity, Sociologist, John L Campbell of Dartmouth College, shows the corrections of Corporations of America in 2009, one of the top private prison corporations in America, owning and running more than 66 prisons at the time across the United States. Theses 66 prisons housed around 75,000 inmates and employees, and 17,000 correction professionals. The privatization of prisons has become a very lucrative business as history has shown. For example, the stock price of CCA climbed from $8 a share in 1992, to about $30 by 2000. Fast forward all the way up to 2017, CCA is bringing in about 1.8 billion dollars a year in profit, a private corporation that has made tons of profit since its opening in 1983.

Another private prison management company, Wackenhut Correction Corporation, enjoyed an average rate of return on investment of 18% in the late 1990s, during the mass incarceration push. It was so successful in fact, that during the late 90's it was rated by Forbes as one of the top 200 small businesses in the country. The private prison industries were sweeping in money all over the country, nearly a decade after its beginning. In 1990, there were just five private run prisons in the country, housing about 2,000 inmates. By the year 2000, there were nearly 20 private firms who ran more than a hundred prisons, with about 62,000 inmates.

Although the number of private facilities increased further, to 415 between 2000 and 2005, and represented virtually all the increase in correctional facilities during those years, there was still many more publicly run facilities. However, a trend towards privatization was evident just as much a decade ago, as it is today. A trend that has been perfected by America's elite. Today's prison systems on one hand, punishes the lower class, especially members of the black community, through bias laws and policies set out to target us. This in return helps populate the prisons.

On the other hand, the prison profits the upper class who own the prisons or who are heavily invested in the stocks, all the while employing the quote on quote, middle-class, who are helping to run the prison. Once they have filtered enough people into the prison system, the next step is outsourcing the free labor they have now acquired, through what you should know are the loopholes in the 13th Amendment, that has allowed the continuance of slavery through the punishment of crime. However, we are not aware of how big modern-day slavery is and how many of our big blue-chip companies participate in it. Here are some names that you might recognize. McDonald's, Walmart, AT&T, Victoria's Secret, Bank of America, Boeing and many more. Whole Foods for example, is a corporation famous for its animal welfare rating, yet apparently was not as concerned about the welfare of humans working for them in Colorado prisons.

In April of 2016, Whole Foods promised to stop exploiting prison labor due to several protests against it. You know that tilapia you thought you were buying from a supposed American Family Farm? When in actuality, they were raised by prisoners in Colorado who are paid as little as $0.74 a day. This goes for the whole milk and fancy cheese too, all produced and processed by prisoners working for cheap labor as well. McDonald's is another, one of the world's most successful fast food franchises, purchases a plethora of goods manufactured in prisons, such as uniforms that were sewn together by prisoners.

Walmart, a place where I even worked summer jobs during my college years. A place whose company policy clearly states that forced or prison labor will not be tolerated by Walmart. Yet basically every item in this store, has been supplied by third-party prison labor. Walmart used to purchase its products from prison farms where laborers are often subjected to long hours in the hot sun, without adequate food or water. Victoria's Secret has used female inmates in South Carolina, to sew undergarments and casual wear for lingerie companies.

In the 1990s, subcontractors of 3rd Generation, hired 35 female South Carolina inmates, to sew lingerie and luxury wear for Victoria's Secret and JC Penney's. In 1997, a California prison put two men in solitary for telling journalists they were ordered to replace made in Honduras labels, on garments that were made in the US. AT&T, one of the leaders of iPhone service, a company well known in the 1990's for finding ways to dump union workers, save big money, and exploit the labor of prisoners all at once, laid off thousands of telephone operators, paying prisoners in their place for their work, only $2 a day. BP or British Petroleum sent a workforce mainly consisting of African American inmates, to clean up the 4.2 million barrels of oil that had spilled into the Gulf Coast, mainly choosing prisoners because of how cheap the labor would be. The spill put many local community fishermen out of work and struggling to make ends meet.

Solving their problems, Starbucks subcontractor signature packaging solutions, hired Washington State prisoners to package holiday coffees, to cut labor costs. These are just to name a few instances. The fact is the list goes on and on. From your well-known companies, to high-level government corporations. Prison labor is still a huge part of the American economic system. Besides the physical standpoint of the inmates, another way the prison system is used in the United States is of course through a form of deception, in most cases to spew numbers.

The prison system can be viewed as an incipient form of active labor market policies, sapping up access labor capacities that might otherwise be unemployed. Remember that the current prison population is not considered unemployed. After all, a great many of the people residing in jails and prisons today in the United States are African people. Young, uneducated and of lower class, who would be among the ranks of unemployed if they were not in jail or prison. So indeed, if these men or women were not incarcerated, they would be unemployed.

For example, the US unemployment rate in the 1990s would have been as much as 2% points higher than it actually was. This does not mean the development of the penal state was solely designed to reduce unemployment rates, especially among the African community to present a better picture of economic growth and prosperity, but it did have such an effect. For example, in a study done in 2014, results show the same as the ones in the 1990's. That the unemployment rate would be much higher for African people in America if you took into account all the men in prison. Using the unemployment rate of black men in 2014, we found that 11.4% of black men were unemployed, not factoring in the native prison population.

This is still a massive number when you consider white men's unemployment rate was only 5%. As a result, making the black men's unemployment rate twice as high as white men, which is mind-blowing, considering the fact that there are two to three times as many white males in the United States as there are black. That number becomes even more mind-boggling when you factor in the men that are due to be incarcerated. According to a 2014 study, if you factor in the number of black males incarcerated, the unemployment rate for black men would have been 18.6% compared to just 6.4%, if you factor in the incarceration rates of white men. That would mean there would be nearly three times as many unemployed African men as white.

Harvard Sociologist Bruce Western writes in his book," Punishment and Inequality in America", "imprisonment makes the disadvantaged literally invisible" from an economic standpoint. Western argues that America has locked up so many people, it needs to rethink how it measures the economy. For some communities such as the African community, the economic consequences have been staggering. According to census data from 2014, there are more young black high school dropouts in prison than have jobs. A lot of that has to do with the public-school system taking the trades out of the schools, in return preparing kids coming out of high school for college, instead of the workforce.

Kids in today's time can no longer do anything with a high school diploma, so they choose not to waste their time, especially if they cannot afford to go to college anyway. This is one of the problems kids in today's time face. Black kids have a graduation rate of only 75% according to the National

Center for Education Statistics. Taking the trades and skills out of the school has been one of the main factors in the school-to-prison pipeline. A lot of us, myself included, had parents and especially grandparents who never went to college and made a pretty good living for themselves. Whether it was working at the factory or the mill. They managed to live a pretty good life off their high school diploma.

My father is a prime example of that. He never went to college. He learned a skill in high school, went to a 7-month trade school to further his knowledge, and received a certification. He was able to provide for us and get us everything we needed, as well as live a comfortable life. All because he learned and developed a hands-on skill that was taught to him in High School. Today's kids don't have that opportunity. It's almost as if they are given a choice between school and prison, which has lasting effects if they make the wrong choice.

For example, 1 in 13 black adults can't vote because of their criminal record. It also calls for levels of added discrimination on the job or in the job market. Harvard studies have shown as well, criminal records are especially harmful to black ex-offenders. Overall, the result points to the importance of rapport building for finding work, something that the stigmatizing characteristics of minority and criminal status, makes it more difficult to achieve. Derrick Neal, an Economist at the University of Chicago and Armin Rick, an Economist at Cornell, also agree that mass incarceration has been the cause of a lot of economic pain and struggle.

The official statistics are "very deceptive, when trends in the fraction incarcerated are changing", says Neal in an interview done by the "Washington Post". You can measure an increasing employment rate or a falling unemployment rate simply because over this period, we've put more of the people who have trouble finding jobs in prison. Can you imagine what the numbers would look like if these men or women had never been arrested? What if they all had jobs, earning wages on par with people with a similar level of education? These are very interesting questions that America must answer.

Now I know there are a lot of white people as well as African people who are saying, what other choice did they have but to throw them in jail. A key question that brings us back to a key point. We talked earlier in the section about the crack epidemic in the black community, as well as the War on Drugs. Drugs that were shipped in to specifically target members of the black community. Not to mention bias laws and policies that were designed to lock us up for having the drugs, which resulted in a case of supplying drugs for us, then locking us up for selling them.

Even with this information being well documented, I can still hear white people saying, "well the only way to get the drugs off the streets and keep the community safe was to lock people up". However, judging by history, I find that very interesting that masses of people, including the highest level of government would think it would be wise to lock up so many black men, women, and children. People who had already been separated due to the hard effects of crack cocaine and many other forms of drugs. Basically, telling them that the solution is to give them the same result as the problem did, which was separating the black family from each other, only this time not in the form of drugs, but in the form of imprisonment. All the government helped to do, was to destroy the black family even further.

Why not try rehabilitation or fixing the system that made black people turn to smoking and selling drugs as a means of survival in the first place? They could have quit redlining the communities which denied black people the ability to create their own economic means of survival, such as starting their own businesses or owning their own homes. How about instead of them approving loans for liquor stores, gun shops or all types of unhealthy fast food restaurants used to poison the black community, they created places of work, such as factories and mills. Jobs that even members of the black community who are not college educated, can participate in to provide the three essentials for their family: food, shelter and water. It's like I have said many times before, the equation is simple to solve. When unemployment in the black community goes up, crime goes up as a result. If unemployment goes down crime goes down.

Every level of government, every white scholar, every black scholar, and historian understands this logic. Black men, women, and children aren't running around committing crimes for the fun of it or because they want too. Most are simply doing it out of a means of survival. The government, along with the mainstream media, understands this. They just choose not to address it, as part of the propaganda campaign I mentioned in the previous section. Yet, if it's white people on the other hand they treat the situation very delicately and as a state of emergency.

Case in point being the state of West Virginia, where up until recently, residents died every 10 hours of a fatal drug overdose. According to the West Virginia Health Statistics Center, the heroin and opioid plague killed at least 864 people in West Virginia alone in 2016. Of those deaths, 731 involved an opioid of some kind. In 2015, there were 735 deadly drug overdoses and 635 of them involved at least one or more opioids. In fact, the heroin and opioid addiction was so bad in West Virginia, that the state itself could not keep up with the funerals, causing many programs, such as the

West Virginia Indigent Burial, to budget 2 million a year, to help cover funeral expenses for families who would not be able to afford otherwise.

It's important to note as well, this is not a new epidemic. This drug problem has been going on in West Virginia for years now. With that being mentioned, you ever heard anybody come out from any level of government and say we have a "War on Drugs" like policies focused in West Virginia? Have you ever heard Obama or Trump come out and say we need to get those criminals and drug addicts off the streets, the same way they talk about the black community in LA, Chicago and New York during the crack epidemic? The answer is no, because we're talking about white people now, not black.

The U.S Health and Human Services Secretary Tom Price said regarding the drug epidemic in West Virginia, "This is a public health issue. This isn't a criminal justice issue". Price also added "if we're just substituting opioid for another, we're not moving the dial much. Folks need to be cured so they can be productive members of society and realize their dreams". Now isn't that something. Look at the language that is being used?

Secretary Price basically said there is no need to lock up these good white folks, they just need rehabilitation and help so they can become productive members of society again. Which begs the question, if only they had kept that same energy when it came to black folks. Yet, let's analyze deeper, I mean why are there so many white people overdosing on drugs in West Virginia? That answer is again simple, unemployment. In March of 2016, West Virginia had the second highest unemployment rate in the US at 6.5%, trailing only Alaska. According to the Bureau of Labor Statistics reported in August of 2015, West Virginia was the only state to experience a statistically significant decrease in unemployment over the previous year losing 19,100 jobs from 2014 to 2015.

Though the coal-mining industries had been hit hard, with jobs in the sector having decreased from 41,000 in 1983 to approximately 18,000 in 2016, according to the Mine Safety and Health Administration, other industries were struck even worse. The Wall Street Journal said jobs in construction and manufacturing had fallen by 23% and 16% since the recession. Proving that the whole unemployment rate to crime ratio doesn't just apply to black people, it applies to white people as well. Only difference between the two, is how the government seems to handle the situation. Allowing one group to rehabilitate and the other to fill prisons for profit. But like they say, this is America.

Conclusion

In conclusion, I hope that the content from part 2 helps to awaken your mind to the new age of slavery and oppression in America. I can't tell you how tired I am of hearing that slavery is over in America and every one of every race has equal and fair opportunities. Not just from white people but from our people as well, who have still yet to release their minds from the lies of white supremacy. It's important that we acknowledge this new age of slavery and oppression, for us to come together and work towards a solution. Solutions that can effectively counter the attacks that are waged against us. Because if we don't, this is a country that will continue to thrive off the enslavement of African people.

Not just by enslaving African people physically on new age plantations, but also mentally, through deceptive warfare and miseducation, making it a necessity for African people to depend on white folks, or as they said in old times

"Massa", for our everyday survival. Now is the time that we must wake up and realize the conditions and society we are living in. The reason being because, if we do not wake up to the fact that we are still at war and nothing has changed, we as a people will make history. History in the sense that we will become the first people who not only participated in our enslavement, but helped to enslave and kill ourselves for not recognizing and understanding the condition we are currently in. Therefore, it is time my African Kings and Queens, to educate and separate, to never forgive or forget.

PART. 3

RELIGION: PUTTING THE SHACKLES ON YOUR MIND

"TRUTH IS A CONTINUOUS EXAMINATION, AND FACT ALWAYS SUPERSEDES BELIEF"

-DR. YOSEF BEN-JOCHANNAN

It is necessary that we all search to find the truth in life. No matter what for, or no matter what the outcome might be. In a world full of lies and propaganda at times it might be hard to find the truth, especially as an African King or Queen in this country; because your knowledge about yourself and where you come from has always been hidden from you. White lies have become so farfetched, they are now creating lies in order to cover up the old ones, putting us in a position, where now belief has become fact. A perfect example of this, is the modern-day western religions many of us subscribe to till this day. Yes, that's right religion, which one can argue is the most effective tool for holding African people around the world down and in a submissive position.

Now I know most of you are at home like "religion, that's the one thing nobody would dare lie about". Well you're wrong. It has been one of the most lied about topics since it came about thousands of years ago. The reason being because the dominant society knows, the one who controls the religion controls the people by putting shackles on their mind. Which is why I ask that you remove those shackles and have an open mind set when reading this section of the book, as I am only trying to give you facts about religion.

I want you to look at these facts however, as food for thought, because I want you to confirm what I'm saying, by doing your own research. I'm just going to plant the seed for you to water as you so please. With that being said, a lot of the information in this chapter will still be hard for most people to swallow, because it goes against a lot of the core beliefs they've had since childhood. Which is why this chapter is not meant to bash or degrade anybody's intellect about their faith system, but to help you finally pull the wool from over your eyes.

<u>The Power of Religion</u>

Let's start at the beginning with the simple question what is religion? The reason why, is because a lot of us African people just say we're religious, based off tradition. We go to church because momma and grandma went to church. We say we're Christians or Muslims because our parents were Christians or Muslims. When the fact is, most of us don't even know what religion is, let alone what denomination we want to join. Which brings us to the question what is religion?

There are several definitions; dictionary.com says religion is "a set of beliefs concerning the cause, nature, and purpose of the universe, especially when considered as the creation of a superhuman agency or agencies, usually involving devotional and ritual observances, and often containing a moral code governing the conduct of human affairs". Which I for one believe is the best most detailed definition of the term religion. Now there are parts of the definition we have to focus closely on. At the end of the definition it says, "often containing a moral code governing the conduct of human affairs". Stating that a belief in a particular religion can justify whether your actions were right or wrong.

Being that most religions claim to be the word of God or Allah, not from any human himself. It also states, "a set of beliefs...especially when considered as the creation of a superhuman agency or agencies, usually involving devotional and ritual observances". This is stating that religion provides a form of symbolism mainly in the form of a superhuman; in most religions being a messenger such as Jesus or Muhammad. This is one thing history has shown us that can be a serious problem when used to control people.

For example, from an African point of view, a religion like Christianity, which is the most popular religion not only in the United States but the world, with more than 2.2 billion people identifying themselves as Christians, is dangerous to African people. This is especially the case when you look at it from a sociological standpoint. Being as I stated earlier that religion provides us with a form of symbolism, which in the case of Christianity, this symbolism is passed off through a white Jesus. A man who can walk on water, provide food for the hungry and do no wrong. This same symbol of a white Jesus, is hung up in 99% of Christian Churches around the country and the world, symbolizing who and what a majority of African people pray and worship to in the United States every day.

I have even seen with my own eyes, African people with a white Jesus tattooed on them. A shining example of something a lot of us don't like to admit, is many of us African people look at white folks as our saviors. Most of everything some of us do in this country revolves around trying to prove ourselves to the white man. For example, when we start making a little money, we run to the white neighborhood. Instead of building up our own. When we have a particular talent such as music, we go out of our way to cross over to the white audience.

You'll even hear artists say, I want to have more crossover music. When we have to make a decision to choose between the white bank and the black bank, we go to the white bank. Like if we bank black our money is going to disappear. Why is this? The reason is because we are always trying to prove our worth to white people.

A majority of us see them as our saviors. This mindset starts with religion. A tool that has been used to control our minds. White people have always known that the first step to controlling African people is through religion. Margaret Sanger, mother of the feminist and eugenics movement, who I spoke about in volume I, said it herself in a letter to Dr. Clarence Gamble.

Margaret Sanger

"We should hire three or four colored ministers preferably with Social Service backgrounds and with engaging personalities. The most successful educational approach to the Negro is through a religious appeal". She said this because she knew just like everybody else, that the key to controlling African people is through religion. See for most of us, all you have to do is show us a white face and say it's the word of God, for us to go along with the program or be submissive. We are the only race of people who get manipulated into praying and worshiping a God who does not look like us.

White people's God looks white, Chinese people's God looks Chinese, Arab people's God looks Arab. Yet, despite our unique history as it pertains to our relationship with white people in America, and the many acts of genocide that we have suffered at their hands, we are still praying to them and adopting their religion. It is amazing when you think about the situation; how certain religions have completely chained the minds of African people. To put it in perspective, can you imagine if you had the majority of Jewish people living in Germany praying to a German God? After all the Jewish community went through at the hands of the Germans. The world would look at them like they were crazy. That's how they're looking at African people right now, like we are crazy.

But that's the power of religion, a tool that can be used as a way for the wolves to invite the sheep to dinner. The dominant religion at the time is also used to dominate the law of the land. As a result, deciding what is good and what is not, through the eyes of that particular religion. With the dominant religion being Christianity in the United States, you will notice a lot of laws and policies are set out to favor its religious context and principles at the time. For example, Donald Trump's new Muslim ban set out to ban Muslims from entering the United States; casting all people who choose to identify with being Muslim, as a possible terrorist.

Another example is back during the 2008 and 2012 presidential election. Notice how a lot of media outlets tried to paint Barack Obama as a Muslim, even though he went out of his way to say he was not. They do these types of things to remind the people that the only way in the United States is the Christian way. Therefore, anyone who is not praising a white Jesus is labeled as a radical or terrorist, because they can't control your mind. Understand, religion has always been used to justify laws and policies.

The power of religion was taken to new heights in 1610, when a Latin American Catholic priest name father Sandoval, questioned the moral rightness of enslaving blacks. Father Sandoval then wrote to the Catholic church in Europe, inquiring as to whether the capture, transport and enslavement of African people were legal activities sanctioned by the church. On March 12th, 1610 Father Sandoval got his answer from Brother Luis Brandon. Brandon responded "Your reference writes me that you would like to know whether the Negroes who are sent to your parts have been legally captured. To this I reply that I think your reference should have no Scruples on this point. We have been here ourselves for 40 years and there have been among us very learned fathers. Never did they consider the trade as illicit. Therefore, we and the fathers of Brazil buy these slaves for our services without any scruples".

See the Catholic church not only approved of the slave trade, but also heavily benefited from it. This letter from Brother Luis Brandon, was used as a tool for any immigrants coming to America, that slavery was justified and approved by the Catholic church. Much so, that a lot of people don't know that the first British slave ship to reach the Americas was called Jesus of Lubeck. They promoted our enslavement as African people through Christianity. Why do you think they have books called "How to make a negro a Christian" or "The religious instructions of negroes in the United States"?

Just look in the mirror and ask yourself why these books necessary if it was not used as mind control. Why was the King James Version of the Bible the number one bible of choice during slavery? Maybe because it was written just before the approval of slavery in 1619 and fed the dominant white society's claims that black slavery was indispensable to their way of life. Insisting that Africans were in the position they were in because God had marked Africans as "Noah's curse of Ham" therefore giving us black skin and making our enslavement to whites justified in the name of God. However, I would be foolish not to mention the other religions that played a key role in our enslavement. We know about the Christians and the major role they played in our enslavement in the Americas, but there was also the Islamic religion. There is little or no doubt, that the first and oldest religious enslavers of black Africans were Arab Muslims.

A 19th-century engraving depicting an Arab slave-trading caravan transporting black African slaves across the Sahara.

The Arab Muslim slave trade of black Africans is so old, it is hard to know the exact date of its beginning. Most historians believe between the years 650 A.D. all the way up until today, between 10 to 20 million people have been enslaved by Arab slave traders. In the book "The Legacy of Arab-Islam in Africa", Dr. John Alembellah Azumah estimates that more than 80 million black Africans died en route between that time period. These Arab slave traders, according to some historians, knew that according to Islam, they were not allowed to enslave newborn Muslims, so it was not in their interest to try to convert enslaved Africans to the religion, since converting enslaved Africans, would mean that their children could be born free by Islamic law. If the Africans were converted to Islam, it would have granted them more rights as a slave. However, there was no guarantee of freedom, nor was it any guarantee of freedom for their children.

The Arab slave trader often targeted African women for sex. As well, they often practiced genetic warfare on African people. Some men were castrated to be eunuchs in domestic service. The practices of neutering male slaves was not only limited to black males. In the book "Islam's Black Slaves: The History of Africa's other Black Diaspora" author Ronald Segal states, "The Calipha in Baghdad at the beginning of the 10th Century had 7000 black eunuchs and 4000 white eunuchs in his palace". Eunuchs, meaning men who may have been castrated.

These were common practices in the Arab slave trade that were always justified under Islamic religion, which led to them spread the Islamic faith in black African communities in order to seize wealth and slaves; something they did through regular military invasions into East and West Africa around 650 AD, continuing all the way until the early 19th century, where they worked hand-in-hand with the Christian European slave trade of Africans. This transatlantic slave trade provided new economic opportunities for exploitation, which drove the Arab Muslim slave traders into overdrive. Unlike the slavery in America, the Arab slave trade was not limited to Africa or skin color. However, a majority were Black African people. None the less, it was still up to date, the longest and most least discussed slave trade in history.

The reason for this is because, we have been disconnected with our African brothers and sisters outside of America. We don't see any connection; we don't understand that African people all around the world, have been manipulated by religion into our enslavement. It was bigger than Muslims and Christians. Other groups such as the Jews were involved too. The Jews involvement in the modern slave trading and exploitation of blacks, has always been a hotly debated topic.

The Jewish religion always seems to take a back seat when it comes to the exploitation of African people. However, as the years have rolled by, the Jewish involvement in the slave trade has begun to surface as well. The 1991 book "The Secret Relationship Between blacks and Jews", written by the historical research Department of the Nation of Islam, highlighted the roles the Jewish Community played, in not only slavery, but Jim Crowism in the Americas; providing evidence and documentation that Jews came to the Americas as slave traders, auctioneers, plantation owners and slave shippers. Along with members of the Nation of Islam, other scholars have also come out and acknowledged the Jewish community's involvement in the enslavement of African people. Rabbi Marc Lee Raphael talks about the Jewish involvement in the slave trade in his book "Jews and Judaism in the United States: A documentary history.

"Dr. Raphael says, "Jews also took an active part in the Dutch Colonial slave trade, indeed the bylaws of the Recife and Mauricia congregations (1648) included an imposta (Jewish Tax) of five soldos for each Negro slave a Brazilian Jew purchased from the West Indies company. Auctions were postponed if they fell on a Jewish holiday. In Curacao, in the 17th century as well as in British colonies of Barbados and Jamaica in the 18th century, Jewish Merchants played a major role in the slave trade. In fact, in all the American colonies weather French, British or Dutch Jewish Merchants frequently dominated". It is important to note as well, this is coming from Marc Lee Raphael, who is a Rabbi, meaning by definition he is a Jewish Scholar or Teacher, one who studies or teaches Jewish law. Therefore, he has no reason to lie about the involvement his people had in the slave trade, because it would have benefited him to do the opposite.

I point this out because I know we have a lot of people in the Black community, who don't believe anything coming from other Black people. Since that is the case, you can now hear it from a Jew himself, that the Jews were involved in your enslavement. Which is shocking to most, because nowadays Jews attempt to pull the wool over the eyes of African people, making us think that they were our allies because they tasted only a little bit of the suffering we've experienced for thousands of years. When in fact, they were one of the main perpetrators benefiting heavily from our suffering. We have discussed the Christians, Muslims, and Jews but what about the Protestant and the Baptist religions?

They have used African people for centuries as well. The Protestant religions in America have always reflected the values of the dominant white supremacist society. Starting in 1619, the Protestant denomination went right along with the dominant white society in the exploitation of African people. Protestant churches along with Baptist churches, provided a center point for white unity and black segregation, especially in the south. Protestants especially, taught many white supremacists and black inferior teachings.

Faithful slaves were taught just like most other religions, to accept their place in life to be obedient to their white Masters, and their souls will find equality with whites in the next world. Even though a few sectors of Protestants in general felt slavery was morally wrong, a majority stayed loyal to the public policy of African enslavement and inferiority. Now as most times, the Quakers seem to get a pass when we discuss the enslavement of African people, because they were one of the only religious groups to publicly denounce slavery. However, they did not openly demand an end to slavery until much later, when they resolved to neither buy nor sell slaves. Yet many accounts during the early days of America, show the Quakers were among the most prominent of the slave traders.

For the rest of society, the moral questions of slavery and race was either ignored or justified, because the church's primary duty was to offer theological justifications for the existence of the big business of enslaving Africans.

African Origins of Modern-Day Religions

Christianity

If you walk into most American homes today, regardless of race, you are going to see some form of a savior in that home. In most cases that savior will come in the form of Jesus. Jesus over the last several hundred years has become this worldwide phenomenon. Making him a symbol of hope to those in need and a beacon of light for those who can't see. Giving him the title by some, as the greatest human being to ever walk the earth. As a result, causing many to follow the Christian way that he so chooses.

But what if I told you that the blue-eyed blonde hair Jesus, that's hanging in your church and in your living room, has nothing at all to do with Christianity? What if I told you that the person, we call Jesus today's real name wasn't even Jesus in origin? What if I told you that Jesus never existed? That the white, blue-eyed, blonde-haired Jesus was and always has been a figment of one man's imagination. Why is it so difficult for us to figure out this information?

As I have said many times before, we have not just been oppressed physically, but our biggest oppression came mentally. In most cases from those who control us every Sunday afternoon in the name of the Lord. It is the white

Christian who has completely deceived you out of your true African spirituality. No more though. I refuse to let my people get led astray any longer. Because we as African people are the gods of the earth.

The Jesus that is hanging up in white and black churches around the world, is really only a concept of African theology. I will have you know that the first white Jesus that you see today, was not painted until 1504 by one Michelangelo, at the request of Pope Julius. It was the Vatican church itself who hired Leonardo DaVinci and Michelangelo to make these false images of Jesus, Mary and God in the likeness of white people. It was also Pope Julius II who commissioned Michelangelo to paint these white images on the ceiling of the Sistine Chapel. Which as a result, has become one of the most Popular tourist destinations in the world. However, what these people don't know, is prior to Michelangelo's image of Mary and Jesus as the Madonna and child, they were invariably depicted with black skin.

These Black Madonnas still exist today, in over 140 churches throughout Europe. The most famous probably being the Black Madonna of Czestochowa, which dates back to 1382 and is still housed at the Jasna Gora Monastery in Czestochowa, Poland.

The Black Madonna of Czestochowa, in Poland

The Black Madonna of Czestochowa has been visited and recognized by several Popes such as, Pope Clement Xl, Pope Pius X and Pope John Paul II. With all three Popes issuing a Canonical Coronation for the icon image. Meaning an institutional Act of the Pope, expressed through a letter in which a personal representative of the Pope to foreign nations, designates a crown towards a Christological image, under a specific devotional title that is being venerated in a particular Administration. In simple terms meaning they have deep respect for the image. There has always been a deep respect among Popes for the African origins of Christianity. Which is why you see images of Popes like Pope John Paul II, praying to the Black Jesus of Angola or German Pope Benedict XVI and Italian Pope Francis I, praying in a private chapel at the Vatican, to a Black Madonna and child.

Pope John Paul II, praying to the Black Jesus of Angola

You have ancient images such as the Concepcion's, by righteous Anna. Righteous Anna is considered the most Holy Mother of St. Anna, who is the mother of the Virgin Mary. In the paintings, it depicts a black Jesus hugging his black grandmother. All of these pictures can be found in the Coptic Museum in Cairo to this day. If you don't believe me, look it up for yourself and check it out. The St. Mary's Zion Church in Ethiopia, which is one of the oldest churches in Ethiopia, as well as one of the oldest churches in the world, has a picture of the Black Madonna and child dating back to the 6th Century, according to Professor James Small. In the 6th Century, Michelangelo wasn't even born yet, and there was no image of white Jesus in sight.

The St. Mary of Zion Church in Ethiopia would eventually give birth to the Roman Catholic Church. Understand the reason these churches and images have been widely visited and accepted among many Priests and Christian Theologians, is because they know it to be true. Even in their Bible they can't hide the truth in plain sight. In the Book of Daniel, it says the hair of Messiahs head would be "like the pure wool of a lamb" and The Book of Revelations likens the Prophet Jesus's feet to, "fine brass as if burned in a furnace". See, the system of white supremacy is very good at hiding the truth in plain sight, which is why when searching for the truth, we always have to investigate the origins in which it came from. This is no different when we are dealing with religion and the origins of Christianity; origins that many hardcore Christian supporters and Theologians are afraid to talk about for the skeletons that could be revealed.

See the story of Jesus, came out of Africa from our great ancestors in Kemet some 4100 years ago, long before anyone mentioned the word Christianity. It started with the story of Ausar, Auset and Heru, the original three African deities, according to our ancestors in Ancient Kemet, who wrote in the language of Madu Neter or what Europeans call today hieroglyphics.

Ausar (Middle), Auset (Right), Heru (Left)

They wrote their story as follows. Ausar was the ruler of Kush, which is presently called Sudan today, just south of Kemet. Ausar was a brilliant leader as well as a genius. Ausar was said to be the developer of the first written language Madu Neter, otherwise known as the language of the Gods. With the development of the new written word, Ausar went to spread his teachings throughout the Nile Valley Civilizations. During his travels, he met a beautiful Nubian woman named Auset, whom he eventually married.

As Ausar continued to travel, his fame and popularity grew as well throughout Kemet. He was considered a unifier, a man of order and virtue. However, Ausar's newfound fame provoked envy and hatred from his brother Set. Set would try his best to tear down the teachings of Ausar word for word. Set continued to do this, until it created mass chaos in Kemet. Yet, it was never enough to stop Ausar.

This drove his brother Set crazy and in an act of pure hatred, Set murdered his brother Ausar, dismembering Ausar's body into 14 pieces and spreading them all over Kemet so they could not be found. When word got back to Auset of her husband Ausar's death, she instantly went into hiding fearing she was next, all while looking for and attempting to recover the missing 14 body parts. During her search, Auset recovered everybody part except one, being Ausar's penis. Using the found body parts of her husband, Auset anointed each body part with oil and wrapped him in linens. In doing so, Ausar's body actually came to represent the practice of mummification and with his green and black coloring, he represented the regeneration of the Earth.

Auset then began to grieve over not just her husband's death, but also because they hadn't yet consummated their marriage, meaning Auset was still a virgin. As legend goes, it was the spirits of Ausar who heard her cries. It was then that Auset became pregnant by an immaculate conception, through the spirit of her dead husband, nine months later giving birth to a son named Heru. Heru endowed with the spirit of his father, was given the mission of defeating his uncle Set, thus restoring order to his father's Kingdom on Earth, as the rightful heir to a unified Kemet. Till that time, Auset lay hiding, fearing that Set would find out and kill the appointed son of Ausar; Heru, who at the age of 12, removed himself from his native population, to go further south into Kemet.

All while in south Kemet, Heru preached of his father Ausar's Kingdom and gathered and prepared disciples for a battle to restore Kemet. He then returned at the age of 30, to battle his uncle. The battle between the forces of Set in the north and the forces of Heru in the South, was epic. In the end, it was Heru and his righteous armies that were victorious. After defeating his uncle, Heru chose not to kill him, but just bind him in chains to the end of time.

After his victory, it was said Heru transformed into a falcon and was called up into the heavens to stand before his father and give testament. Ausar was very proud and pleased of his son so much, that he blessed him and sent him back down to earth to rule as the true leader of Kemet. This also in return made Ausar the God of the underworld. To commemorate the victory of Heru, every single Temple and Royal House in Kemet carved a winged sun disk otherwise known as the Heru Bedet, above every entrance. This Heru Bedet, served as a reminder of the virtues of order and a warning against the dangers of intemperance and jealousy.

This was just a summary of the ancient theological Kemetic story. Several great books to read to get the full and detailed story are "African Origins of Major Western Religions", "The Egyptian Book of the Dead" and "The myth of Genesis and Exodus" to name a few. I want to remind you as well, that this was written some 4100 years before there was anybody by the name of Jesus. These original ancient Kemetic teachings, set the blueprint for many of the religions we see today like Christianity, Judaism, and Islam to name a few. Many took copies of the story or at least, took bits and pieces.

For example, let's start with one of the more basic symbols you will see today. When you go to ancient Kemet (Egypt) today and look in the tombs in temples, you will see an Ankh.

An Ankh the Kemetic symbol for Life

At first sight you will see that it closely resembles what we know today as a cross. The difference being the loop at the top, that some call a Nubian cross. This image was embedded in rock long before any religious concept was tied to it. The ankh frequently appears in Kemetic Tombs, often with the fingertips of a God or Goddess holding it in the image, representing what many scholars believe to be the life after symbolizing conception. The Christians and other religions groups simply took the same symbol and used it to their liking.

The Christians, after stealing the representation of the Ankh, used and flipped it into a representation of Jesus dying for our sins; a way of Christians trying to make their cross seem more relevant and original to their religion, when they know they got their design from Kemetic origins. As well as, many scholars and historians are starting to figure out the cross that we see today depicted by the Catholic church itself, can be found in ancient Kemet. Long before Christianity existed, on the walls of the temples of Abu Simbel and Philae, even in places like Nubian and Kush. Unfortunately, scholars and historians have never been able to decipher what the symbol means. Nonetheless, our ancestors gave us the first concept of spirituality and a divine spirit.

Ancient Kemetic teachings taught us, in the beginning there was Nun, the primal waters which one might even describe as matter. Then out of Nun would rise Amun, which represents the unknown, the unknowing factor that allows something to come into being. Then out of Amun would rise Amun Ra, meaning the light, energy and radiation. Amun Ra would then produce Shu and Tefnut, basically meaning air and moisture. When the air, moisture and minerals would combine, it would give birth to Geb and Nut. Geb was considered the Earth and all the minerals that it makes up.

Nut was the sky, meaning all elements of the atmosphere including the stars, moon, planets and even life itself. The combining of Geb and Nut, gave birth to an Ausar and Auset. Meaning that all human beings would come forth from the elements of the earth and the energy from the sky.

This would then become the blueprint for others to copy in their creation story. Thus, when they talk about Adam. they are referring to Geb talking about the Earth. When they talk about Eve, they're talking about Nut.

Eve is representing the energy and life that comes about the elements of earth, like Nut. Now the question becomes, how did we lose this history about ourselves? The answer is simple, we live and have lived for hundreds of years, under systematic white supremacy. The same goes with religion. Thus, when Kemet was first seized by the Greeks in 332 BC, they were so amazed by the city, that the first thing they tried to do was claim it as their own, by changing the name.

Like we talked about in volume one, all the conquerors of Kemet did, was change the images and the names of previous African symbols and culture, to make it their own. They blew off the noses of monuments like the Sphinx and converted all Kemetic language to Greek, which was a major sign of disrespect. It's like calling somebody outside their name. Eventually that name is going to catch on and everyone will begin to pick it up and before you know it, no one even knows their real names. That's why I make a conscious effort throughout this book to call our Kemetic monuments, spiritualities, kings, queens and etcetera by their real name, in order for us to understand our history properly.

See the reason why most of you have never heard of Ausar, Auset and Heru, is because their names have been changed so many times. Starting with the Greeks, who changed Ausar's name to Osiris, Auset's name to Isis and then Heru's name to Horus. The second name change came when Rome took over Kemet from the Greeks, around the time of 30 BC, after the death of Queen Cleopatra and with that came new names. This is where the first form of Christianity started to take shape. The mythos of Osiris became known as the Holy Ghost or the Holy Spirit.

Isis became who we know today as the Virgin Mary and last, but not least, Horus became known as Jesus, which becomes even more obvious when we start to analyze the story of the two. Osiris begins to take shape as the Holy Spirit, by the Roman Catholic Church, who impregnates a virgin through an immaculate conception. The story of the Virgin Mary would be a copy of the story of Auset, or as the Greeks would call her Isis, therefore following the same storyline of becoming impregnated through an immaculate conception and giving birth to a son. Jesus would be the Christian version of the original Kemetic savior Heru, who would come back to lead his people. The Kemetic version says Heru and Auset fled to southern Kemet, to hide from Ausar's brother Set, because Auset feared he would kill Heru.

In the King James version of the Bible it says, "and when they were departed, behold the angel of the Lord appeared to Joseph in a dream saying, arise and take the young child and his mother and flee into Egypt and be thou there until I bring the word: for Herod will seek the young child to destroy him". Now we know both Heru and Jesus fled at the birth, in fear of getting killed. Furthermore Heru, during his time in Southern Kemet, teaches his disciples to gain followers. As the Christians tell it, Jesus too began to spread the word of God to his 12 disciples and so on. The same twelve disciples that Jesus handpicked himself and were the foundation of the church to carry on after Jesus. Well just like everything else. Kemet had their original twelve disciples as well, known as the Neteru. Heru, Set, Thoth, Khnum, Hathor, Sobek, Ra, Amon, Ptah, Anubis, Ausar and Auset.

All of their names were representative of nature and each of the functions and characteristics of the disciples are presented in everyone's human development. That's what the people of Kemet thought spirituality was supposed to do, help one gain knowledge of self and spirituality. To give you the tools to develop any one of the multiple strengths of the Neteru that the Christians called Disciples. Even today in Kemet, you have the Coptic Church, which is one of the oldest churches in Kemet. Located in Cairo, it is believed in Christianity that the Holy Family once visited and stayed at the site of Saints Sergius and Bacchus Church.

A church that dates all the way back to the 4th century. Interestingly enough, in the Cairo Museum they have one of the oldest paintings of Jesus and his 12 disciples and guess what color they are? Black, because they knew the very exact place where they stole it from, the people were jet black Africans, but I digress. It was Heru who returned back to Kemet to defeat his uncle, in order to bring Kemet back to prosperity and fulfill his father's goals. In Christian circles, you have Jesus who also returns to his people to die for their sins and fulfill his father's goal of making the people a believer in God. If you are still not a believer, that the connection is real between Heru and Jesus, then look no further than the several scholars and historians such as Dr. Jabari Osaze, Dr. Kwame Nantambu, Joseph McCabe and more, who have confirmed the fact that Heru's birthday was always celebrated in the temples of Kemet on December 25th.

Joseph McCabe documented in his book, The Story of Religious Controversy "every year the temple of Horus presented to worshipers in mid-winter (or about December 25th), a scenic model of the birth of Horus." Now as you can see, no story 2000 years apart can be this similar. I think it's safe to say that most English teachers in America, when comparing the two stories, would come to the conclusion that one simply plagiarized the other, plagiarizing that took damn near a thousand years to complete, when you look back at history. We know this from the documented Nicaea councils. Councils that were started under Constantine in 325 A.D. in order to gather the collection of stories to rewrite the bible.

It would then take from 325 A.D. to 780 A.D. just to get a single Bible that was universally agreed upon. In other words, it took over 400 years and 7 councils for them to change and modify the story of Ausar, Auset and Heru. We don't even get the first Catholic church until 1054 A.D. Now once they had formed the church 40 years after that, the first thing they did is put together an army to invade the Middle East in 1095 A.D. This is an important fact that many scholars fail to realize. The Army would then become known as the Crusaders, who under orders by the Pope Urban II, would attack the Muslim forces in the Holy Land of Jerusalem. Thus, 4 years later capturing it in 1099.

As you can see, the minute these white supremacists got some information from Africans, they flipped it and attacked us with their war machines. Then it wasn't until the 15th century, that we get the reformation from Martin Luther, that produced the Methodist Church, Baptist Church, Episcopal Church, Evangelical Church etc. Then in 1529, Henry VII of England, separates from the Roman Catholic Church and creates another form of church, all as a means of control, recreating the so-called word of God as they see fit, to push whatever agenda they had planned to get the masses behind it. It is important to know that there was no such thing as Christianity and ancient Kemet. The Kemetic spiritual teachings of Ausar, Auset and Heru were just considered a way of life.

As you can see, the Europeans took it and turned it into a religion used to control the mind. There were no such things as black Christians in Ancient times, the black Christian was made at the end of a gun, a sword and in most cases a whip.

Judaism

Christianity is not the only religious group that has historically stolen and rewritten African history and achievements. Judaism and its followers have also helped to participate in this destructive process, changing our history and spirituality as a people, through religion. For example, till this day we continue to have Jewish rabbis and priests who tell lies, that the Jews built the pyramids. Their religious holy text, the biblical Book of Exodus, claims the Jews built the pyramids as slaves in ancient Egypt. They even took this lie as far as Hollywood in the movie "Exodus Gods and Kings", which featured an all-white cast, making one ask the question, did the Jews really build the pyramids. After all, who would spend so much time and money projecting a false statement?

The Jewish community that's who. Because the evidence just doesn't add up. Now according to Jewish biblical text, Abraham is considered to be the first Jew. A man who came into existence around 1800 B.C. roughly because unfortunately the Torah does not give dates. That would put Abraham's life span around the 13th Dynasty in ancient Kemet; which is important to note, because most scholars and historians, such as Dr. Yosef Ben Jochannan, agree that the pyramid dynasties were between the 3rd and the 11th Dynasty, or between 2613 BC and 2010 BC. Pyramids in this timeframe include the Djoser step pyramids, as well as the Pyramids of Giza.

Step Pyramids of Djoser 2667 - 2648 B.C. (3rd Dynasty)

So, my question to Jewish Rabbis and Priests is, what pyramid did you build? How can you build something when you haven't even been born yet? This is physically impossible wouldn't you agree? As well, there is no documented record of any enslaved people building the pyramids in ancient Kemetic history. Something just doesn't add up, but I'm sure if you mentioned this to any Rabbi or Jewish Priest, you will just be labeled as anti-Semitic, which by the way doesn't make sense, because black people are a Semitic people in origin.

The original Semitic people were people from northeast Africa, especially Ethiopia, who the father of European history Herodotus described as having thick lips, broad noses, woolly hair and being burnt skin, but I digress. As we continue to go down the list of myths and lies, we now stop at Abraham's most important Prophet, Moses. He is most famously known as the prophet of Abraham's religion, who brought the Israelites out of slavery. A man, who according to Jewish text, received the ten commandments from God himself. It said in the Book of Exodus, that Moses led his people to Mount Sinai, where Moses on the seventh day, went into the mountain for 40 days and 40 nights and on his return, came back with two tablets.

On the tablets were the ten commandments, said to be written with the fingers of God himself, making for a very popular story in modern day culture. Yet one must ask, is this story true or more plagiarism? I remember myself, when I was young, singing songs about Moses in the Elementary School chorus, believing every word of the song. Looking back on it, that's how they get us. I didn't know any better.

In my mind, Moses saved our people and gave us the words of God. However, the truth always finds you, along with the whole story. See what they don't tell you, is that Moses was born and raised in Kemet. According to the Hebrew Bible, Moses was even a former Egyptian Prince. Now if Moses was a real person who grew up and was raised in Kemet as an Egyptian Prince, he must have heard and known of the 42 negative confessions. After all, they were taught in every school and ancient Kemet at the time.

In "The Book of Coming Forth by Day" (The Book of the Dead), in the Papyrus of Ani, is the negative confessions.

Papyrus of Ani in the Tomb of Ani – 1250 B.C.E

The forty-two gods and goddesses of the names of Kemet conducted this initiatory test of the soul before the scale of Ma'at. Ma'at being the Goddess of truth, balance, order, harmony, law, morality and justice. These confessions are translated in the book of the coming forth by day otherwise known as "The Egyptian Book of the Dead " by EA Wallis Budge. The 42 confessions state I have not murdered, I have done no harm, I have spoken no lies, I have not defiled wife or any man, etc., just to name a few of the 42. Now don't these confessions sound familiar to the Ten Commandments that Moses supposedly got from God.

I'll say it again. Are you telling me that a man who was born and raised in Kemet, went to school in Kemet, who the Hebrew Bible said was even a prince of Kemet, never heard of the 42 negative confessions? Confessions that can be found in the temples of Seti I, in Abydos and in the Tomb of Ramses III till this day. Confessions that were written thousands of years before anybody wrote about a man named Moses, who supposedly went up to Mount Sinai and got these commandments from God. On top of this it is important to remember that Moses is not a literal figure but a mythological figure. Therefore, many of Moses's supposedly claimed works and writings, were in fact pseudepigraphy. Meaning that these works where falsely attributed works whose claimed author is not the true author.

Islam

Islam, just like Christianity or Judaism, has an African origin as well. Yet just like Christianity and Judaism, the Islamic spiritual system has been whitewashed in order to hide its African origin. As a result, leaving some to believe that the religious teaching of Islam comes out of the Arabian Peninsula from the mind of the pale Arab. This could be no further from the truth, based on the evidence. Evidence that concludes that Islam first and foremost, predates Muhammad, who is the seal of the messengers and prophets of God in all the main branches of Islam.

A man that many credit with starting Islam and giving birth to the name Allah, the highest and most supreme God. Yet, the only problem with this theory, is the word Allah predates Muhammad as well. According to Arthur Jeffrey in his book, Islam: Muhammad and his Religion, he states that "The name Allah...was well known in pre-Islamic Arabia. Indeed, both it and its feminine form, Allat, are found not infrequently among the theophorous names in inscriptions in North Arabia". We also have physical proof of this, for example in Sumatra Harabesi, in the Tektek mountains located in Edessa, Syria.

Where at an Arab sanctuary, the people left an inscription dating back to 165 C.E. reading as follows, "I, Tiridates, son of Adona, governor of 'Arab, built this altar and set up a pillar for Mār 'Allāhā, 'Lord Allah", 400 plus years before the so called birth of Muhammad. Facts are, evidence of the worship of Allah in ancient Arabia, has been found in both the northern and southern portions of the Peninsula, mostly leading back to the Lihyan tribe in Northern Arabia, where scholars found hundreds of inscriptions dating back as far as 500 B.C.E, invoking the name Allah pre-Islam. These Lihyanite inscriptions invoking Allah as God, were written by the Banu Lahyan, a subgroup of the Hudhayl. According to several scholarly works such as Black Arabia & the African Origin of Islam, by Dr. Wesley Muhammad, the Hudhayl people were described by their complexion. In the Encyclopedia of Islam, it states "Their skins were black and shining" when referring to the Hudhayl. These were the people who made up the original population of Arabia.

We have to remember that no matter where we go in the world, the original people of that land were African. This is no different when it comes to the Arabian Peninsula. First of all, we have to note that the Arabian Peninsula is nothing more than an extension of northeast Africa. An extension that over the last 200 years, has falsely been reclassified and identified as the Middle East. This term and idea of a Middle East, is based strictly off of the imagination of white Europeans, which is why the term was originated out of the British India Office of London; which named the land after its geographical location as it pertained to them, in the middle of Europe, Asia and east of Britain. The term would later be popularized by Alfred Thayer Mahan, an American naval strategist.

However, in "The Emerging Picture of Prehistoric Arabia: Annual Review of Anthropology" Maurizio Tosi states, "this trapezoidal (Arabian) peninsula is the geological continuation of Africa...Physically, the peninsula is a part of Africa, landscaped by the same geological and climatic processes as the eastern Sahara and the Ethiopian highlands...In general Arabia is the continuation of the

African system across the Red Sea." So, we're clear everything that has come out of ancient Arabia including Islam, is considered an African contribution to the world, for Arabia is Africa and was populated by African people. In the book "African Presence in Early Asia: 1st Edition" Dr. Runoko Rashidi gives us more proof of this as he states, "The Arabian Peninsula...was, like much of Asia, first populated by Black People...Some of the surviving black populations, known as the Veddoids, are major portions of the Mahra population found still in the extremities of Arabia."

Mahra man of the Arabian Desert Yemen.

These are the people who introduced the foundations of Islam, these are the people who lived at the time of Muhammad and fought against white Christians in the crusades. As Rotholandus, the Frankish military leader under Charlemagne said when referring to the black Muslims of the time, "Hoarders blacker than the blackest ink...no shred of white on them except their teeth".

African Spirituality in
Western Culture & Hollywood

We talked about the African origins of today's modern religions, but what about the African spirituality that makes up pop culture and Hollywood today? African spiritual symbols and figures that have been whitewashed and diluted in order to hide their true meaning and origins. For example, let's start with the eye of Heru, otherwise known as the Eye of Horus.

Eye of Horus

Due to T.V. stations like the History Channel and shows like Ancient Aliens, whenever we see the eye of Heru, we automatically associate it with freemasonry or the Illuminati. Powerful groups of old white men, who secretly control the world through these symbols. When in fact, the eye of Heru is an Ancient Kemetic symbol, representing the one who sees everything that is going on down below. Personified in the Goddess Wadijet, who is considered one of the earliest

Kemetic Deities. You will see the eye of Heru depicted as some type of Illuminati symbol but this notion is false.

First thing to note is that there are two eyes. The left eye symbolizes the eye of Heru or Wadijet, which you can find on the one-dollar Bill floating above a pyramid. The founding fathers of the United States did this to pay homage to Kemet, who they modeled the United States after. The Kemites derived the eye out of the story of Ausar, Auset, and Heru, where according to the story, Heru himself transformed into a falcon and flew up into the heavens to stand before his father. Heru, with a falcon head symbolized his ability to fly over and hear and see all. The myth goes on to say that Heru's eye was damaged so badly during the battle with his uncle, that it had to be repaired by the God Thor.

The restored eye became known as Wadijet, referring to the left eye representing the moon. The right eye is known as the eye of Ra representing the Sun. These two images are commonly used and seen in many Masonic lodges and other rituals around the world today, but the original images represented the falcon God Heru, watching over Kemet. In "The World's Eye" by Albert Potts, he states that as far as religion goes, the association with an eye on the dollar bill did not emerge until well into the Christian era.

The Eye of Providence

The eye surrounded by the triangle, was an explicit image of the Christian trinity. The Christian trinity that we know, ties back to the original three deities Ausar, Auset, and Heru. The Eyes of Heru and Ra, were drawn thousands of years before there were such things as Masons, Illuminati, or even the Eye of Providence. However, let's keep going down the list of religious ideas and symbols that were stolen. Often times, in America we are calling upon and using African spirituality without even knowing it.

For example, one can conclude that 79% of Black America calls upon a God of Africa every night before going to bed and twice on Sundays, by saying one simple word at the end of every single prayer, Amen. Yet somebody told them a lie that it meant "so be it" when it never meant so, be it back in ancient times, nor does it mean it to this day. Amen was the God of the north, north Kemet that is. Ra, symbolizing the sun, was the God of south Kemet. When they unified the north and the south, they unified the gods as well, creating the God Amen Ra or Amun Ra.

In many of the ancient Kemetic temples, they would

always chant out Amen, paying homage to the Kemetic God. In Revelations 3:14 Jesus calls himself the Amen. Jesus is trying to identify himself as the Kemetic Sun God. They also say in Matthew 13 and 14, Mary and Joseph took the child to Egypt to fulfill the prophecy "Out of Egypt I called my son", meaning Jesus believed he was the sun God who unified Egypt. Yet, many religious scholars and theologians will tell you that this is just a mere coincidence, that two spiritual systems, thousands of years apart, just so happened to call upon the same name to deliver their prayer. I mean how stupid do they think we are?

You know, I find it funny though, how after all of these years of white people telling us we were inferior, telling us that we were a people who had no history, were dumb, stupid and slow, yet these same people have always called upon our God to deliver their prayers. See family, this has never been by coincidence, it's always been a part of the plan. Ask these so-called theologians, scholars and historians. Is it by coincidence that the Vatican City for example, which is the heart of the Roman Catholic Church, has a Tekhenu (Obelisk) in the middle of St. Peter's Square?

The Kemetic Tekhenu in St. Peter's square

Unfortunately, little is known about the origins on which Pharaoh constructed the Tekhenu, but it was certainly quarried in Kemet. It is believed that sometime between 30 and 28 BC, the red granite Tekhenu, shows up in Alexandria under Augustus. It was Gaius Caligula, who had the Tekhenu brought to Rome in 37 A.D. It was the largest non-inscribed Tekhenu to leave Kemet standing at 25.5 Meters high and weighting an estimated 326 tons. Now I want you to stop and go back and remember what I told you the first Tekhenu was built for in "Voice of the Ancestors VI".

It was built to honor the first mythological king of Kemet. Ausar, a shining symbol of his resurrection. This is important because we know that the Romans conquered Kemet from 30 BC to 646 A.D., meaning that for approximately 700 years, Romans ruled Kemet. However, on the flip side Popes and other members of the Roman Catholic Church, want you to believe that they never heard of Ausar, or why the Tekhenu was built to honor him. Please family, do not fall for this scam, they knew exactly who Ausar was and that's why they put the Tekhenu in the middle of St. Peter's Square in the Vatican to not only honor Ausar, but to honor the African origins of Christianity. The Tekhenu located in St. Peter's Square is just the most well-known and recognized of the group.

There are several Tekhenus located all around Rome, 13 of them to be exact, which is more than anywhere in the world including Kemet. All of the Tekhenus in Rome were brought to Rome by various Roman emperors, which goes to show you how much they know and admire Kemetic culture. Like I said earlier, there isn't one Pope in the history of the Roman Catholic Church, that doesn't know the story of Ausar, Auset and Heru. As stated in "Voice of the Ancestors VI" there are also Tekhenus in Washington DC,

Paris and elsewhere. Therefore proving, that what you have is a worldwide phenomenon based off a single culture. However, African Spirituality in western culture goes far beyond architecture, money, or even Kemet. Our African spiritual systems are portrayed in Hollywood on the big screens as well, only under different names. A classic example is the Orishas of the Yoruba spiritual system.

Illustration of Orishas gods from the Yoruba spiritual system.

Many of the Orisha deities have been portrayed in Hollywood movies, especially ones dealing with superheroes, only without proper credit or respect given to their African origins. Take the X-men comics and movies for example, where damn near all of the superheroes in the series are based off the orishas. Superheroes such as Professor Charles or Professor X as he is sometimes called, is depicted to be the founder and leader of the X-men, people who are seen as having deformities or being mutant. His superpower is that he can control people's minds through conscience. They got this concept from the Orisha deity Obatala, who is the father of the Orishas and all children who are handicapped or have deformities. He is also the owner of all heads and the mind, controlling people through conscience.

Next you have the superhero Storm, who is played by Hallie Berry in many of the X-men movies. Storm has the power of mother nature, she controls the winds and hurricanes, strikes the lightning and creates the tornados. These powers make Storm one of the strongest X-men. Her character is based on the Orisha deity Oya. Oya is the Orisha of winds, lightning, violent storms, death and rebirth. She is a warrior and is unbeatable in combat.

Then you have Wolverine aka Logan, who is the warrior X-men, known for his animal-like fighting skills. When he is angry, three machetes come out of each hand in times of war. This concept was built off the Orisha deity Ogun. Ogun is the Orisha God of war, iron and labor. He is always the first one used for war and is almost always depicted with two machetes, one in each hand. In fact, in the 1988 Wolverine comic series, Wolverines mentor, who first showed him how to fight, was a mutant name Ogun.

Ogun on the cover of Kitty Pryde and Wolverine

Solid evidence that the tie between the Orisha and the Marvel comic book series X-men, does in fact exist. However, not just limited to the X-men, certain members of the Avengers also have an Orisha overtone to them. Thor, for example, who is the God of lightning, storms and strength. A God who is oftentimes seen in Marvel movies wielding a double-sided hammer or axe. His character is damn near identical to the Orisha Shango.

Shango rules over lightning, thunder, fire, the drums and dance in the Yoruba spiritual system. Shango is probably the most well-known and popular, out of all the Orisha and is always depicted or represented with a double-sided axe. All in all, these are just a few of the many heroes that have an African counterpart or origin. The word hero in itself, came from the Kemetic word Heru, which was translated into hero at the hands of the Greeks. Just one of the many words and ideologies that have been stolen from your African spiritual systems.

<u>Conclusion</u>

As you can see through the evidence, I have provided in this chapter all the religions that evolved out of Africa. Now I understand that many of my religious kings and queens reading this chapter, will either be one or two things after reading this. Upset or confused, both are good. If you are upset, or if I have offended you in any kind of way, I am happy. Not because I want to rub it in your face or embarrass you, but happy because I hope it encourages you to go out there and do your own research to attempt to prove me wrong. That is the whole goal of the Voice of the Ancestors series, to inspire others to do their own research and not settle for the popular opinions that are pushed on to us in school.

If you are a member of a church, go challenge your Minister or Bishop about the word of God. Ask him if he knows about your faith system's relationship to African spiritual systems. I'm sure most of you will be surprised by the answers. Because one of the biggest problems we have as a people, is being afraid to ask these critical questions in fear of the answer we may receive. Any church that tells you, you shouldn't challenge the word of the church, is not a church you should be a part of.

A wise man once told me, people never get upset when confronted with questions they can answer with factual evidence, because they can prove it without a doubt. However, the questions they can't answer with any type of factual evidence, they will answer with myth or force, in order to make you a believer. Last thing to remember when you are asking these questions, is the reason why you are asking them. You are asking them essentially because the God inside of you wants to know. The God in you is always searching for the truth, which is the very reason you are reading this book now. Because the God in you brought you here. It's like the old saying goes you can't hide the truth because the truth will set you free.

PART. 4

QUEEN QUEEN

SHOW ME HOW YOU TREAT YOUR WOMEN, AND I'LL SHOW YOU THE CONDITION OF YOUR RACE.

- DR. YOSEF BEN JOCHANNAN

As I was writing this book, a book that was meant to inform and educate members of our community not just in the United States, but around the world. A book that was specifically speaking to the younger generations of Black kings and queens, the 90's babies and the millennials. I felt as if I would be doing a disservice to my people, if I did not enlighten them of the treatment of the Black man's most prized possession, the Black woman. That's right, our most prized possession. So often when we talk about being robbed of our knowledge of self, the first thing we normally think about is the cultures we lost, our achievements that were stolen from us, or our African spiritual systems that have been disconnected from us as a whole.

All these things are extremely important. However, when we talk about being robbed of a knowledge of self, no one seems to ever mention being robbed of what it means to be a human. Our traits for compassion, love, and kindness have all been sucked out of us for the most part, not towards our oppressors however, even through slavery, Jim Crowism, mass incarceration etc. For the most part we still show compassion, love, and kindness towards the people who don't deserve it. You see, we lost what it meant to be African.

In return, we lost the reason for and behind our existence, our black Queens. At one point in time in our great history, we cherished her and held her up as a shining example of what beauty was. Our queens such as Nefertiti, were known in ancient times to be the most beautiful woman to ever live. However, black women throughout history haven't just been known for their looks, but for their bravery and courage as well; like Queen Amina and Harriet Tubman. Black women such as Betty Shabazz, who witnessed the murder of her husband Malcolm in front of her eyes, yet still had the courage and bravery to shelter her kids under the bench and shield them with her pregnant body.

All of these traits and more, live in our strong black women to this day. Yet some of us don't want them for a wife anymore. We have called her out of her name so many times, she has responded to it and accepted it as her name, embracing the ignorance that has been instilled on to her. We the Sun people have started in many ways, to develop the characteristics of the Ice people when it comes to our Queens. This must change if we want to restore ourselves as a race of people.

We cannot move forward by leaving our most prized possession behind. In this chapter my sole goal is to uplift and reunite our Black queens worldwide, to the place where they rightfully belong, which is by the black man's side. As a result, we will discuss some important history and facts regarding our queens, that will help to uplift them and educate black men on how they should be treated and respected. It's time to give our Queens the attention they rightfully deserve.

The Black Woman is God

Growing up as a young black man in America, I would say 75% of the things I heard or saw about black women were negative. Yet it wasn't until my sophomore year in college, when I realized how far the black man has been separated from the black woman, as well as how little we understand about our women. I will never forget, I had just gotten out of football practice, when one of my college teammates told me, "Chase, I'm done with Black women". When I asked him why, he said "black women aren't anything but trouble, white girls are pure, they don't have all that drama". As appalled and disappointed as I was in my brother's statement, I couldn't even be mad at him. For the simple reason that, this mentality was instilled in him and other brothers through systematic white supremacy.

A system that pushes the miseducation of young black men in the school system and in the media. To even think of the black woman as trouble and the white woman as pure, is a form of sickness in itself. I'm in no way trying to disrespect the white woman, but how can you say a white woman is purer than a God. That's right a God! There isn't one race of people on this planet, that did not come from the black woman at one point in time.

The black woman is truly the mother of all humanity. If you remember in Voice of the Ancestors VI, Part 1, we talked about Mendel's Law, which again states that a dominant gene can produce a recessive gene. However, two recessive genes cannot produce a dominant gene. In simple terms, with black skin being a dominant gene and white skin being a recessive, there is no way two white people can give birth to a black person. Yet two black people can give birth to a white skin person.

This explains scientific evidence and studies such as the mitochondrial eve, which is the matrilineal most recent common ancestor of all current living beings, tracing all the way back to a black woman who lived in central Africa. Mitochondrial Eve is where all living humans descend from; in an unbroken line, purely through their mothers, and through the mothers of those mothers, back until we converge on one woman, a black woman who lived roughly 200,000 years ago. Now since we know, according to many scientists and scholars, that the white race is only 6,000 to 8,000 years old, this means for the 192,000 years prior to the white woman, there was a lineage of black Goddesses giving birth to her race. So, on a biological level, the black woman is God, making her the Mother of all human beings and civilizations, we seem to have forgotten that in today's age and time. See we spend so much time in America talking about racism and rightfully so, that we don't talk about the sexism that is embedded in that racism.

Don't get me wrong, the main priority has to be race first for black people. Yet we wouldn't be fans of intelligence, if we didn't pay attention to how racism and sexism play hand in hand, as a result impacting and fragmenting the world as we know it today. Why is it that 99.9% of all religions we as a people are associated with, are praising a man? Have you ever stopped and asked yourself that question? Why isn't the woman held up and looked at as a God, even though many of these biblical stories are myths and written in allegory.

Why is it that the man, is always the one who is praised

and worshiped? The reason being is because, under the system of white supremacy, over the years we've associated the strong male-like figure with being the only deity worth praising, despite the fact that, anybody with any common sense will be able to tell you that you cannot have a God without a Goddess. Even in the Catholic Church, for all my brothers and sisters who are Catholic, in the prayer Hail Mary, it says "Holy Mary, Mother of God". Yet I've never heard any Christian in prayer ask Mary for help. If you pray to Jesus as if he was a God like figure, wouldn't that make Mary a God too? Because last time I checked, both Jesus, Muhammad, and the many other Prophets and god-like figures, had mothers, all of whom were proclaimed, but never mentioned.

The person who created you is the God, which in origin would be the black woman we all trace back to. We in this generation, have lost that knowledge. Keyword being 'we', because our ancestors knew. Again, going all the way back to Kemet with Ma'at. Ma'at was the Goddess of truth, justice, balance and morality. Ma'at was represented as a black woman to our ancestors in Kemet, symbolizing the concept of balance and order. She was the one that kept the stars in motion, the seasons changing and the maintaining of the order of Heaven and Earth.

The people of Kemet believed that Ma'at was the way to reach the afterlife, because she would be the ultimate deciding factor. It's important to remember that the people of ancient Kemet did not have a religion, but a way of life. They lived by the laws of Ma'at, which was represented in the 42 negative confessions that we discussed earlier. "I have not committed sin, I have not stolen, I am not a man of violence" and so on; all of which were eventually chopped down at the hands of Europeans to form Moses's 10 commandments which he claimed to be the words of God.

However, they were really the laws of Ma'at, the black woman. Meaning in Kemetic culture, living a balanced life of justice, harmony, peace and beauty, was represented in a black woman.

Ma'at is also where the Greeks derived the word math, the concept of finding the equal or balance of something. Looking deeper, we continue to see the importance that the black woman played in our ancient cultures and civilizations. When you look at Auset or Isis, the mother of Heru, her name means "throne", symbolically meaning that as a black man, you can never reach the top without the Black woman, because she makes and is the throne you are inspired to sit on. We get our salvation through her. One of the first Gods ever created in Kemet, was the Goddess Tefnut.

Tefnut was the goddess of rain, air, moisture, weather, fertility and water. As well to add to them, you have the Gods Geb, Nut, and Shu. You have Geb, who was said to be the God of Earth. Shu, who was the God of the wind and air and Nut, who was the Goddess of the sky and heavens. You can find drawings and depictions of these three in all the coffins and temples of Kemet, with the Geb laying on the ground, Shu standing with both arms out to the side pointing at the breast and vagina of Nut, a black woman.

Geb, Nut, and Shu photographed by the British Museum

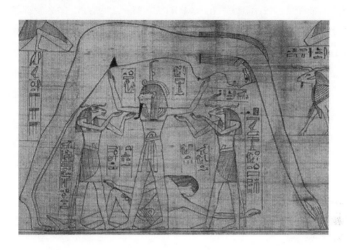

The reason for this is because our ancestors were describing to us, since Nut was the Goddess of the sky and heavens, that her breasts and her vagina is where you can experience heaven on earth. This is coming from the greatest civilization the world has ever seen. A civilization whom we owe our mathematics, science, music, astronomy, etc. too. They said that how you treat the black woman and honor her principles represented in Ma'at, would be the deciding factor if you were going to heaven and if you wanted to experience heaven on earth you could experience it through her too. Yet moving forward, let's not just focus on Kemetic beliefs.

Let's look at others too, who in silence pay homage to the black woman. When you look at Islam or people of the Islamic faith, one thing that is clear is their devotion to Allah. You will hear Muslims say, "Bismillah Al-Rahman, Al-Rahim." Meaning in the name of Allah, the most compassionate, the most merciful. In Arabic, what they are saying is they are seeking mercy by the way of Allah's womb.

Because if you ask anybody who speaks any form of Arabic, not just African people who have just adopted the religion without learning the language, ask them about Rahman or Rahim and the Triconsonantal root of the R-H-M. The triconsonantal root of the R-H-M means "womb". In case you don't know, the womb is the uterus in a woman or female body, in which babies are conceived from, by definition. Meaning in Islamic faith, you're seeking mercy or refuge by the way of Allah's womb. Now if Allah has a womb, what does that make Allah? The answer for any person of intelligence would be a woman. Which makes sense, because when you look back at pre-Islamic Arabia including the one in Mecca, they prayed to the Goddess Allat.

The word Al-lat, was used as a name or title for multiple pre-Islamic Goddesses of Arabia and was used for either the wife of Allah, or daughter depending on the region. In Mecca before Islam, the Quraish tribe worshiped three female deities; Allat, Al-Uzza and Manah, while for the Nabateans, Arab people of Petra and Jordan, Allat was seen as the mother of all Gods. Yet if man was to find out that God was a woman, his ego would be hurt. Therefore, we continue to push the alternative narrative, especially in the Middle East Islamic States or countries where women are treated like second-class citizens.

For example, Saudi Arabia is a place where women have just received the right to drive in 2018. Yet they still cannot make major decisions without male permission, like interacting with men without a time limit, or just going for a swim in a public pool. See the dominant male figure in these cultures, wouldn't be able to handle the fact that their God is a woman. It would shake the very ground they walk on, because no matter what religion I go to, Islam, Christianity, Judaism, they all at one point in time worshiped the black woman.

Just look at the Popes from the Vatican, who are still going around the world kissing the feet of the Black Madonna and child. Yet we as Black men, still have yet to grasp her worth. We have not only misunderstood what she means to us spiritually, but physically as well. The Black woman was the first one we had to rely on for nutrition, both inside and outside her stomach. She was our first protector from harm's way. If she was to fall down the stairs, put the wrong thing in her body or become too stressed out, many of us would not be reading this book now.

She is your first yielder, she is your first sustainer, and she is the merciful one, while at the same time, she is the one you pray on for mercy. Take the most basic definition of God provided to us by the Merriam Webster online dictionary. It says God is, "one controlling a particular aspect or part of reality". As well, it's important to know that God is a neuter noun, meaning denoting or belonging to a gender of nouns, which for the most part have inanimate referents, or do not specify the sex of their referents. I say that, because in a male dominated society, we have naturally over time associated the word god to a man, when the term can be appropriated to either a man or a woman, which makes perfect sense, when you go back to the definition of God "one controlling a particular aspect or part of reality".

Now who was the initial creator of your reality, before you were introduced or could understand any form of religion? Remember it is the black woman who took a sperm, nurtured it and cared for it for nine months, in order to deliver a child who after, provided colostrum fluid, a form of nutrients from the breast, that all newborn babies need. The colostrum fluid that enhances the psychology of the child, the immune system of the child, as well as the digestive system of the child. Meaning that child got something from their creator that they couldn't get from anywhere else, going all the way back to our original creator being the Black Woman. As Brother Polight says, "that is having autonomous control over something specific to an aspect or creation". Meaning the black woman, was the first God of your universe as you knew it.

Now with that being said, I am in no way trying to diminish the role or importance of the black man, for the black man is a God in his own sense. The problem comes in when we have brothers in our community who will say the black man is God, yet when I say the black woman is God, they look in disarray. Common sense should tell you, if you the black man view yourself as a God which you are, and if she has the ability to produce and persuade a God, what does that make her? I know brothers who will travel across four states just to receive her blessings. This is why it's time for us to wake up.

Not just black men, but black women as well, seeing that you have the gift of persuasion. As a black woman, you have the ability to help awaken the brothers with your presence alone, because we all know that no one can get a black man motivated like a black woman. We need our Black women to push us and hold us black men accountable for being conscious and having knowledge of one's self. Go back to the Civil Rights era in the 50's and 60's, where the black woman made it cool for a black man to be conscious and embracing the whole black empowerment movement. Brothers back then sometimes we're just joining the Black Panthers or nation of Islam just to have some form of knowledge of self, for the simple fact they knew that's what black women liked.

Fast-forwarding to today, black women have let black men off the hook. Not forcing the black man to treat himself like a God, has in return forced you to diminish your status as one. Not all black women however, but for the most part, many black women have told the man he doesn't have to be a God anymore. You made it cool for him to be a black man with no knowledge of himself, just an athlete. You made it cool for him to have you, then two or three other women on the side. You made it cool for him to call you outside your name and treat you any kind of way.

Now I would never say that you hold the sole responsibility of the condition of the black man today. We as black men must take self-responsibility for our actions as well. However, you the black woman being a God on earth, have to quit allowing it to be acceptable for the black man to develop a money over everything mentality. Money over consciousness, money over the community, even money over you. Therefore, you have a job of helping to restore the black man along with the black family as well, because as you go, we go.

The black woman is the most important part of our existence as human beings, that's where the black man becomes God, because we are children of her. We have to stop believing all these myths. That God fashioned Adam from dust, then took one of Adam's ribs and made Eve. If we claim to be people of intelligence, we have to leave behind these fabricated stories and deal with reality. We have to get back to putting the black woman on her throne, because the black woman is God.

The Black Trinity

Unfortunately, in today's point in time we are at a handicap in the Black Community. The reason being, up until now there has always been a war to separate and tear down the black family. Separating black fathers from their sons through the legal system, in order to make that boy grow up fatherless, seeking attention from any male figure, trying to find it in the dope man on the corner, or the miseducated negros he sees on T.V. As a result, straying down the same path his father did, ending up in jail or ending up still having characteristics of a child, because he never learned how to be a man, the side effects of never having a father figure there to teach him. Yet up until maybe the last 20 to 30 years, all of the primary forces for the most part fighting to separate the Black family, were external forces.

Forces that in one way or another weren't our fault. However, fast-forwarding to today, the forces separating us are not only external, but internal as well. Meaning, we understand that mass incarceration is still a problem in 2020, as well as economic traps set by the government, such as redlining but what about us? In the Black mind in 2020, mentally white supremacy has kicked into full affect. This is due to the new age of social networks and how the black family is betrayed by the mainstream media, offering a new threat to the black family.

One that has developed internally in the minds of black people, one that has changed the game for white supremacy. Because you have to remember, although we have been living under the system of white supremacy for over 400 years here in America, the war on the black family has never been as detrimental as it has been in the last two or three decades. Even during 200-plus years of slavery, the black family was still essentially strong. Even during 150 years of Jim Crowism, the black family was still strong. The black man and black woman were still together happily married, because back then we knew all we had was each other.

With that being said, one of the reasons I feel as if the black man and black woman are so divided to this day, is because of the way we tend to portray our struggle. For example, when we speak on some of our most influential black leaders, we see pictures with Malcolm X and the iconic shot of him with his finger pointing to his head. We will also see similar pictures, like that with Fredrick Douglass, Marcus Garvey, Elijah Muhammad, Nelson Mandela and many more of our great freedom fighters. There is no doubt about it, these were great men. Yet, what these pictures don't show, is behind every great man is a great woman. We rarely show you or tell you about Anna Murray Douglass, Amy Jacques Garvey, Betty Shabazz, Clara Muhammad, or Winnie Mandela.

Anna Mary Douglass

Amy Jacques Garvey

Malcolm X and Betty Shabazz

Elijah Muhammad and Clara Muhammad

Nelson and Winnie Mandela

The wives of Fredrick Douglass, Marcus Garvey, Malcolm X, Elijah Muhammad, and Nelson Mandela. I bring these Queens up because when you see those isolated pictures of our Male Freedom Fighters that I mentioned before, they are always being depicted as our freedom fighters by themselves, separate from their family and separate from their kids. Their images are always hung up without you ever seeing their female counterpart. If I show you a picture of these Queens, you probably will not even know who they are. When in fact, they were right there by the sides of some of our most influential black leaders.

These Queens were even out in the streets with their partners, facing white supremacists, dogs, tanks and water hoses. Their lives and the lives of their children were threatened on a daily basis, just like their significant other. There is no coincidence that behind all of these strong black men, are strong black women, which is important to know, because in today's society we have the tendency to make the fight for Black Liberation about the black man to a certain degree. Therefore, making the fight for freedom, an isolated man struggle, versus white supremacy. When in fact, the fight for liberation is for the black man, woman, and child. Meaning the black family as a whole, is a part of the fight for liberation, a fight we will never win without the black woman by our side.

The best teacher of our community is the black woman. The Black woman has always been able to convey messages to the people we as males may not be able to deliver. That's why our ancestors said if you teach a male, you teach an individual, if you teach a woman you teach a nation, understanding that the black woman is going to make sure that the message reaches to the next generation and beyond. We must get back to our most basic African ideologies that the black man, woman and child together, are the original three deities. We are in spiritual terms Ausar, Auset and Heru, the original Holy Trinity or Family. Therefore, to restore our godliness in order to liberate our community, we need to reunite the Black family.

One of the keys to making this happen is getting back to

the concept that " Black men must date and marry Black women and vice versa, Black women must date and marry Black men". It is as simple as that. There is no way you can convince me that you have the best interest for your community when your male or female counterpart is of another racial community. Let me tell you why, it is because you are telling your people that your standards for excellence is outside your own community. Who you marry is one of the most, if not the most, important decision you will ever make, both politically and economically. Who you marry tells me who you are.

For example, take me. If I Chase McGhee, married a white woman, I'm not only marrying her, I am marrying her culture, community, her people and her beliefs. That would be me sending out a clear message to the community, where and who my standards of excellence lay with. I'm telling you that the culture, people and beliefs of another racial community are more important than my own. See, there is no greater symbol to who you are than your wife or husband.

There's no greater symbol of your loyalty to your community, than to marry somebody from your community. There is no greater symbol of what you value and prioritize the most, than your wife or husband. Now let me answer the obvious question many of you are itching to ask and that is, "you can't help who you fall in love with, right?" Wrong, because love is not blind, but simply a function of the values and prioritize in your life. This is just like anything in life.

People value and prioritize keeping their body healthy, so they make sure they go to the gym or the doctor's office. Despite the fact most people hate doing so. You value and prioritize the health of your teeth, so you make sure you go to the dentist. That doesn't mean you love the dentist, it's not about love, it's about what you value and prioritize. In a 2017 report done by the Pew Research Center, it showed that black men are twice as likely to marry outside their race as black women.

The Pew research also shows that since the 1980s, the amount of interracial relationships in America among Black people has more than tripled. That's more than any other community but why is this? It's not because of love, but for the same reason that affects us when it comes to politics and economics. Which is why ironically, who you marry is both a political and economic decision. Because black people in America as I have said time and time again, are in love with status symbols.

We think somehow by marrying the white woman or white man, that this is going to move us up higher on the social and racial hierarchy. Unfortunately, we find out the hard way that it does not. For most of us, marrying the white woman or white man is a symbol of us making it, which is sad. We treat marriage just like we do any other situation. The whiter it is, the better. Get a little money, what do we do? We move into the white neighborhoods. When we get a chance to transfer our child to a white school, what do we do? Move our child to that school.

I've spoken to black women who have told me that they want to marry a white guy just so their baby would not have nappy hair. They weren't joking either. You got black men out here who are dating white women and love to talk about how nice her parents are and how much they like you. How she never argues with you like the black woman. My brothers stop it.

These white folks don't give a damn about you. Some of the same brothers who say this, date black women and treat them like dogs, then turn around and get a white woman and treat them like Gods. We in the Black Community almost do as much stereotyping about ourselves as white folks do. Again, we must regain some knowledge of ourselves. My queens stop throwing every black man into one category because you had one bad experience.

I can't tell you how tired I am of seeing the bashing of black men on social and mainstream media by black women who have had a bad experience. Especially when there are plenty of good brothers out here who are educated, hardworking, and who cherish and love black women. This is why the law of attraction is important. Now when I say attraction, I don't mean from a physical standpoint of how you look, because all sisters and brothers are beautiful in their own way, both inside and out. When I say the law of attraction, I am talking about from a mental aspect.

Being your ability to attract into your life what it is you think about or focus on. This is why you hear many of history's wise men say you are what you think about all day long. So, if you keep believing and telling yourself that "black man ain't s***" or that "black men aren't good for anything" those are the type of Black men you are going to attract. Think negative and you will always get negative results. Think positive and you will always get positive results no matter how long it takes.

However, it starts with how you shape the consciousness inside your head, about how you want your husband or wife to be. The Law of Attraction will take care of the rest. The same thing applies to my kings as well. We talked about in the last section, that the black woman is God, therefore we must stop degrading her. Being a man of understanding, realizing that the black woman has seen a lot and been through a lot.

She might prejudge you from time to time but stick with her and stay persistent with her if she is the queen for you. Prove her negative pre-judgements wrong with the respect and love you show her. Even if it doesn't work out, be a black man she can trust and count on in the future. Most importantly, don't ever bad mouth her to anyone else. It doesn't matter how long or short or how good or bad the relationship was, as black kings we never bad mouth our queens, especially not on a public platform.

Just be thankful and appreciative of the lesson learned from that situation, wish them the best and move on. Never disrespect another god, because that will only create more friction between us as a people. The further apart the black man and woman are from each other, the weaker we will be as a community. The closer we are, the stronger we are as a community. We don't realize how powerful of a statement it would be from a powernomics and social standpoint, seeing the black family together.

For example, I'm not an Obama fan, but I thank him and Michelle for showing what a black power couple look like. The image that they created will be priceless in the minds of young black kids growing up today, reminding the children, that you can be a strong successful black man, with a strong black woman by your side, or that you can be a strong black woman in politics, with a strong black man by your side. This is important because we saw shows like Scandal, that gave the impression that the only way that a black woman can move up at her job, is to sleep with a white man. We see shows like Empire, where nearly every black man in the show has a negative relationship with the black woman in some way form or fashion. Even when you look outside the community, most times our children are shown the black athlete or Entertainer with a white wife or husband.

Another example is LeBron James has a beautiful black wife but when is she ever talked about or put in the mainstream media. Again, most of us probably don't even know her name. Yet when is the last time you went a day without hearing about Kim and Kanye. We must promote and push for more black power couples in our community, and it starts with the individual black man and woman. Now that was from a social and political standpoint.

Let me tell you where economics comes in. Marriage in many ways is a business transaction, especially when you talk about one individual making a more significant amount than the other. Which is most likely the case when you talk about our black professional athletes. Marrying outside your race can mean a transfer of wealth from one community to another, whether it works out or not, but especially if they don't, because studies have shown that divorce courts are big business, generating between 50 to 175 billion dollars a year; while weddings just generate 40 to 50 billion dollars annually. Tiger Woods former wife Elin Nordegren walked away with close to 100 million dollars after their divorce in 2010. Do you think she gave some of that money back to the black community for her come up? After all, when she met Tiger Woods, she was a nanny.

Nonetheless, let's just say your situation with your white counterpart is different, everything works out fine and you live happily ever after. The question is how long though is happy ever after for the black man? Studies show on average, the female is expected to live longer than her male counterpart, leaving all of your wealth and assets to your wife. If you are a Black man married to a white woman, do you expect her to give a damn about the black community once you are gone? Probably nine times out of ten all that wealth will be transferred to the white community.

This is why it is important that you marry in your race from an economic standpoint, because the ones who will benefit most from this, are the future generations of black children. See, the ones who deal with racism the most, are the ones who are considered biracial by no fault of their own, because one cannot decide who brings them into this world or how they got here. But when you have children with members from another community as parents, you put pressure on that child to bear the brunt of that. Your child is now viewed as not black enough, but not white enough on the other side. The word "biracial" in itself, was used to divide us in general, creating a sort of civil war in the black community.

Now you have black women like Megan Markle and Amber Rose, talking about I'm not black I'm biracial. However, we know in the system of white supremacy you cannot be the slave and the slave master, so it creates a confusion among our black children, forcing them to be outcasted or forcing them all together to completely disassociate with one group or the other. What makes it even worse, is we have two different parents coming from two different perspectives in life. I don't care how many black men or women, he or she has dated, they cannot tell you what it is like to be black. There is no way a parent from any other community can understand that child's struggle.

The one black parent of the child will probably sugarcoat the struggle because they married outside of their race. So, they may tell the child something like, "racism doesn't exist", which is one of the worst things you can tell a child. Racism affects everybody in all walks of life, whether good or bad, young or old. That's why it's best to have two parents who look like the child, to help them encounter that everyday struggle. Again, let's be clear, as black people, we are at war.

There is no way around it, and it is nothing new. If you have a biracial child, help them to understand that they will be viewed as black. They will not get the benefit of the doubt if the cops pull them over. To tell them anything different will be handicapping them. Trust, love, compassion, protection, and honesty is what we must give our children, starting with the black man and woman giving it to each other, then spreading that love down to the next generation, recreating that holy bond which would make us indestructible.

Her Wrath

Religion has always been a powerful tool used to control the masses. When you go to churches nowadays, you will hear the Preacher try to incite fear into people. Reason being in order to make them do what the preacher wants them to do. You'll hear them say if you don't do x, y, and z, you will feel the wrath of God. Well, being that the black woman is a God, we have felt her wrath on several occasions throughout history, from both a mental and psychological standpoint, but as well from a physical standpoint.

I told you earlier that in today's society, especially within the conscious community in particular, we are so quick to point out black men who have fought for our liberation, but never black women. I'm not just talking about the black women who stood by and supported their man and family, but the black women who throughout history stood alone as well. Black women who picked up arms and fought and even died for the liberation of our people. Black women who maintained and sustained empires that were ahead of their time. Black women who were overthrown and exiled from their kingdoms by colonizers, for fear of her divine power. Yet never receiving the proper recognition they deserve for the role they played in our history.

For example, a lot of people today when they think about the Black Panthers, just think about a whole bunch of brothers who took up arms and challenged the system of white supremacy, with a few sisters in the background supporting them. Yet a lot of us don't know there were more women in the Black Panther Party than men.

According to a 1969 survey by Black Panther chairman Bobby Seale the Black Panther Party was over 60% women.

Women like Assata Shakur and more, who were on the front lines involved in shootouts as well. This is just one of the many examples of the role that black women played in our revolutions throughout history. Daniel McGuire, an Assistant Professor of History at Wayne State University, argues that armed self-defense, was also far more common for black women in the south, than has generally been acknowledged. In Maguire's 2010 book, "At the Dark End of the Street: black women, rape, and resistance", McGuire contends that the decision by women to combat sexual abuse and violence, sometimes with force, was one of the sparks that led to the modern day Civil Rights Movement. Therefore, meaning that the wrath that was felt by the United States by our black women, was one of the reasons some change finally came. Yet these are things they don't want you to know, in order to paint the non-violent picture that keeps us submissive today.

While in the 60s, they were trying to make it seem as if

black men were the thugs raping black women, when in fact it was the opposite that was going on among white men, forcing the black woman to defend herself. This is not uncommon when you look throughout our history. Black women have not only been the ones to stand up and fight for liberation, but in many cases the first to do so, using her voice and her actions to awaken the masses of lost Negroes. That is why throughout the rest of this section, we will look at some of the most influential and fearless black women throughout our history. Black women who built, sustained, and maintained empires across the world, and who were not afraid to put their life on the line for their people, from past to present.

Queen Amanirenas (Reign 40 BC - 10 BC)

Queen Amanirenas was an African Queen from the Kingdom of Kush which is now located in modern-day Sudan. She was known as the Kandake, meaning great woman or queen mother. A name given to her by the indigenous people of the land. She is mostly remembered for her military courage and genius in battle, especially against the Roman armies that occupied Egypt at the time. Around the time of 30 B.C., Roman armies had complete control of Egypt and were looking to take their reign down south into the kingdom of Kush.

They did this by attempting to put a tax on the Kushites, but the Kushites refused, leading to a five-year war with the Romans. During the early years of the war, Queen Amanirenas' husband was killed, therefore passing the reins of the Kingdom to her. Much to the Roman's surprise however, Amanirenas wasted no time avenging her husband's death, as she quickly destroyed the Roman occupied city of Syene sacking and vandalizing statues of Roman Emperor Augustus in the process. The course of war between the Kushites and the Romans would go back and forth over the next few months, with battles so brutal that Queen Amanirenas would end up losing her eye in one, leading the Roman Governor of Egypt Gaius Petronius, to refer to her as the "one eye queen". After several months of fighting in a stalemate between the two sides, a peace treaty was eventually settled on.

As a result, unlike other Kingdoms near Roman territory, the people of Kush were never enslaved, forced to pay tribute, or give up resources to the Romans; all because of the efforts of Queen Amanirenas and her troops.

Queen Yaa Asantewaa 1863-1923

Yaa Asantewaa was named Queen Mother of the Ejisuhene, part of the Ashanti Confederacy, which is now part of modern-day Ghana. She is one of the most loved and praised figures in Ashanti history and the history of Ghana, due to the stance she took when confronted by colonialism from the British, who had captured their King Prempeh I and exiled him to the Seychelle Islands. In order to get him back, the British wanted the Ashanti people to surrender their historical, ancestral golden stool, which was a dynastic symbol of the Ashanti Empire, a symbol that would have been seen as a token of submission by the Ashanti people. British Colonial Governor Frederick Hodgson, also said at the town hall meeting in front of Asantewaa rulers, he wanted to sit on the Golden Stool as a symbol of British power, which was a total disrespect to the Ashanti people. At the time, Queen Yaa Asantewaa was the gatekeeper of the golden stool. Therefore, when she heard the talk from some of the fellow rulers about surrendering, she made a speech that would boost her into legendary status.

Queen Yaa Asantewaa said "now I have seen that some of you fear to go forward to fight for our King. In the Brave Days of Osei Tutu, Okomfo Anokye, and Opoku Ware, leaders will not sit down to their king taken away without firing a shot. No white man could have dared to speak to a leader of the Ashanti in that way the governor spoke to you this morning. Is it true that bravery of the Ashanti is no more? I cannot believe it. It cannot be! I must say this, if you the man of Ashanti will not go forward, then we will. I will call upon my fellow women, we will fight the white man. We will fight to the Last of us fall in the battlefields".

Her epic speech motivated the Ashanti people and led to the Ashanti-British war of the golden stool, led by Queen Yaa Asantewaa and an army of 5,000 troops. During the war, Queen Yaa Asantewaa was eventually captured and deported, but not before her bravery started a kingdom-wide movement to get King Prempeh I back and to win their independence.

Nanny of the Maroons (unknown - 1733)

The Jamaican people have always been known for their resistance against slavery. For this very reason one of their most heroic figures in their history is Queen Nanny of the Maroons. Queen Nanny was born in what is now present-day Ghana, to the Ashanti people, a people known for their war like culture. It is unclear how she got to Jamaica, but it is believed that she came as a slave herself. However, her slave status was shortly lived, as she quickly escaped the plantation in which she belonged to and ran into the mountains and jungles of Jamaica. Thereafter setting up a place that would later be known as Nanny Town and leading a group of escaped Africans known as the Windward Maroons.

During her lifetime, she helped to set free more than 1,000 slaves, through a numerous number of successful raids on European plantations, kicking off one of the longest wars in Jamaican history, the first Maroon war that lasted 18 years. It is believed by some historians and scholars, that Nanny was killed in 1733 during one of the many bloody battles that ensued in the war. However, as some Jamaican oral traditions teach, the real Nanny was never killed, because during those times, everyone was called Nanny for strategic purposes, which is one of the biggest reasons her name still lives on today in Jamaica. Her life and accomplishments have been recognized by the Government of Jamaica with statues and awards in her name. She is currently the only Jamaican National Hero who is a woman.

As well as the only Jamaican woman who is featured on a currency, the $500 note. Which is one of the largest banknotes in Jamaica.

Sanite Belair 1781 – 1802

If you're looking for a story of courage and bravery look no further than the story of Sanite Belair. Sanite Belair was a lieutenant under Toussaint Louverture during the Haitian Revolution. A revolution that was the first of its kind in that the native slave population successfully rose up and overthrew their oppressors. Sanite Belair was a big part of the success that would later come from the revolution, in that she was known to have led many uprisings. It is said that together, she and her husband Charles Belair are responsible for the uprising of nearly the entire enslaved population of Artibonite, against their enslavers. Leading general and future Haitian ruler Jean Jacques Dessalines and many more to refer to her as the "Tigress of Haiti" for her ferocity.

However, after being wanted by the French for quite some time due to insurrections, Sanite and her husband Charles were eventually captured and sentenced to death. Sanite by decapacitation and Charles by firing squad. Yet, Sanite refused, she fought and fought with the French insisting that she dies with honor, the same way as her husband by firing squad. After getting her way, the French attempted to blindfold her, but she refused again. She walked to her death with bravery, courage and respect.

Then finally, when the time came, she looked at her fellow Haitian brothers and sisters who were forced to watch and shouted "Viv Libète anba esklavaj!" (Liberty, no to Slavery) as they fired. Words that helped to fuel and continue the revolution to victory. Even to this day she is still seen as an inspiration and a hero to the Haitian people. As her legacy was cemented in 2004 on the 10 gourds, making her only the second woman in history to be featured on a Haitian banknote.

Queen Nzinga 1583-1663

Queen Nzinga, the Monarch of the Mbundu people, is probably my favorite queen of all time, for her courage and bravery in times of challenge and controversy. During the late 16th century, out of fear of the French and English, the Portuguese had been forced to search for slaves in different parts of Africa. As a result, after establishing relationships in nearby Congo, the Portuguese then turned to Angola, just south, establishing a fort and settlement just outside Mbundu land, leading to several negotiations and accommodations between the Mbundu and Portuguese people. Queen Nzinga however, noticed the Portuguese were trying to control their land as a whole, pressuring the Mbundu people into the slave trade. Queen Nzinga as a result, being the brilliant chess player that she was, formed alliances with former rival states.

She led her army against the Portuguese, initiating a 30-year war against them. Queen Nzinga was very intelligent.

She exploited European rivals by forging an alliance with the Dutch and with their help, Nzinga defeated a Portuguese Army in 1647, when the Dutch were in turn, defeated by the Portuguese the following year and withdrew from central Africa. Even at the age of 60, Queen Nzinga continued her struggle against the Portuguese, going as far as to lead her troops into battle herself. Her guerilla style attacks on the Portuguese armies would continue long after her death and inspire the ultimately successful 20th century resistance against the Portuguese, that resulted in the Independence of Angola in 1975.

Queen Dahia Al-Kahina 688-705 A.D.

In 639 A.D., a new conquering force swept into Africa. The Arab Invaders had conquered Kemet, Cyrenaica, and Tripoli, and pushed on to Carthage and Numidia. These new conquerors spread Islam from Kemet to Morocco and also into Spain. While doing this, the Arab Invaders also destroyed and enslaved many Africans, causing others to flee further south to evade their clutches. When Kuseila of Mauritania resisted, he was killed in 688 A.D. making Queen Dahia Al Kahima, the new leader of the African Renaissance and one of the bravest and most courageous queens in our history.

History describes her as having "dark skin, a massive hair and huge eyes" referring to her hair may refer to an afro or perhaps dreadlocks. Dr. John Henrik Clarke describes her as a nationalist who favored no particular religion. This may explain her effectiveness and bringing everyone together to form a united front against the Arab invaders. She counter attacked the Invaders and drove them into Tripolitania (Libya). This was so effective, that some Arabs doubted whether Africa could be taken.

The Arabs seized Carthage in 698 A.D., where Dahia defeated them and instituted a scorched-earth policy to prevent the Arabs from being able to find crops to feed on in the region. Eventually, the Arabs returned and Queen Dahia was finally defeated in battle in 705 A.D. and north Africa was overrun. Black people are now a minority in north Africa, and furthermore, Africans in Mauretania, Sudan, and Libya, continue to face the threat of Arab enslavement to this day.

Harriet Tubman 1822-1913

I'm sure many of you have already heard of Harriet Tubman. Yet, I could not leave her out, for the simple fact of how much she did for our people. Arguably the greatest freedom fighter of all time. Harriet Tubman, after breaking out of her shackles and chains, stopped turned around and went back and led 13 more missions to rescue approximately 70 slaves, maybe even more. She also helped white abolitionist John Brown, recruit men for his raid on the Harpers Ferry and found enough courage and heart to take on the Confederate Army during the civil war, becoming one of the best scouts for the Union Army, leading bands of soldiers through the marshes and rivers in south Carolina and other states.

She was able to map out unfamiliar terrain and identify where enemy locations might be based on the layout, later working alongside Colonel James Montgomery, providing him with key intelligence that aided the capture of Jacksonville, Florida. As a result, becoming the first woman to lead an army assault during the Civil War. One of my favorite quotes from queen mother Harriet Tubman, when asked about how she did it was, "I had reasoned this out in my mind, there was one of two things I had a right too, Liberty or death; if I could not have one, I would have the other".

Sojourner Truth 1797 – 1883

Born in Ulster County, New York, Sojourner Truth was sold into slavery at the age of 11 for $400 and a flock of sheep. She was sold four more times after that, until she finally walked to freedom in 1826, carrying her infant daughter, Sophia. She eventually settled in New York, where she took up preaching. She traveled around the east and Midwest, preaching for human rights. This illiterate ex-slave was a powerful figure in several national social movements, speaking forcefully for the abolition of slavery, women's rights and suffrage, rights of freeman, temperance, prison reform and the termination of capital punishment. Gaining many supporters such as Frederick Douglass and more.

One of her big accomplishments that caught the nation's attention, was when she learned that her son Peter, had been sold illegally by Thomas Dumont to another slave owner in Alabama. In a bold and brave decision, she decided to take the issue to court. A black woman taking a white man to court was unheard of at the time and something that seemed very risky. However, in 1828, after months of legal proceedings, she got back her son who had been abused by those who were enslaving him, making Sojourner one of the first black women to go to court against a white man and win her case. Sojourner also delivered some famous speeches during her lifetime. Speeches such as "The Spirit Calls Me" and "Ain't I a Woman".

Along with that, she has been the recipient of several awards and honors, becoming the first black woman on earth, with a bust in the U.S. Capitol, as well as being included in the Smithsonian Institution's 100 most significant Americans in 2014.

Ida B. Wells 1862 – 1931

Ida B Wells was one of the earliest activists for the liberation of black people after slavery. Born in Holly Springs, Mississippi, Ida was forced to grow up at a young age. Losing both of her parents to the yellow fever epidemic, she was forced to raise her brothers and sisters in order to keep the family together. She was a Rosa Parks before Rosa Parks, and then some. She was a strong intelligent and fierce black woman, who in 1884, at the age of 22, fought a white train conductor because he was trying to forcibly remove her from the seat on the train, even though she had a ticket. Ida B. Wells was a queen who mostly made her wrath felt through her powerful voices and journalism skills.

Any injustices committed against black people, Ida tried to make sure the whole world knew about it, and that the perpetrators would be held accountable. In the 1890s, she documented lynching in the United States. She showed and proved that lynching was often used in the south as a way to control or punish black people who competed with whites, rather than being based on criminal acts by black people as was claimed by whites. She provided a voice for black people who didn't have one, earning a fearless reputation, despite numerous efforts to intimidate her including death threats. Ida is also considered one of the founders of the NAACP organization that is still alive today, to ensure the political, educational, social and economic equality rights of all persons, and to eliminate race-based discrimination. Ida B Wells was a relentless force in fighting for our liberation.

Septima Poinsette Clark 1898 – 1987

Septima Poinsette Clark is perhaps one of the only women to play a significant role in educating blacks in America for full citizenship rights, without gaining sufficient recognition. This is the same beautiful black woman that Martin Luther King himself called, the mother of the movement. She is also referred to among many activists and historians, as the queen mother or grandmother of the civil rights movement in the United States, born second in a family of eight children in Charleston, South Carolina, to a lawn dresser and former slave. Education was always a struggle to pay for, but she always found a way. By teaching in segregated schools in various locations, she earned a bachelor's degree from Benedict College in 1942 and a master's degree from Hampton Institute in 1946. She played a significant and underrated role in the Civil Rights Movement, doing what she does best, teaching and educating.

Clark not only taught young students but held informal literacy classes for adults as well, pushing several education and equal rights agendas in organizations such as the Young Women's Christian Association, Federation of Women's Club, the NAACP and more. When she lost her job and pension, for refusing to comply with South Carolina state law, banning membership in the NAACP, Septima was hired by Myles Horton, to become the Director of Workshops at the Highlander Folk School in Tennessee. After being absorbed by the southern Christian leadership conference, Septima and her cousin created the first citizenship school to educate blacks in literacy, state government, and election procedures. Septima traveled through the south, training teachers for citizenship schools and assisted in SCLC marches and protests. Martin Luther King acknowledged Septima, when he received the Nobel Peace Prize in 1964, by insisting that she accompany him to Sweden. Septima Clark, was essentially the architect behind educating the masses of our people on how to vote.

Martin Luther King Jr. and Eleanor Roosevelt, both spoke at the Highlander Folk School and Rosa Parks was a student there before her bus boycott. The impact of Septima, was felt far and wide to help educate the masses of mis-educated blacks in America.

Ella Josephine Baker 1903 – 1986

Born in Virginia and raised in North Carolina, Ella Baker would grow up to be one of the biggest behind the scenes components to some of the biggest organizations and civil rights leaders. She was one of the founding members of the young Negroes Cooperative League in Harlem in 1930, whose goal was to develop black economic power through collective planning. As well, she worked behind the scenes of organizations such as the Southern Christian Leadership Conference, Student Nonviolent Coordinating Committee, the NAACP and more, causing her to work alongside many famous civil rights leaders of the 20th century such as W.E.B Dubois, Thurgood Marshall and Dr. Martin Luther King Jr., while at the same time, mentoring many emerging activists such as Daine Nash, Stokely Carmichael, Rosa Parks, and Bob Moses. Can you imagine what it would have been like to organize all these protests from these different organizations and civil rights leaders? Who decided where to rally? Who got all the permits for the rally?

Who prepared bail for all the arrests? Who called the

media, wrote the speeches, or got the message out to tell everyone where to be, because there was no social media back then? I'll tell you who, that person was Ella Josephine Baker. Pulling all the strings to make sure everything went just right.

Dr. Frances Cress Welsing 1935-2016

Born in Chicago, Illinois, to a father who was a physician and a mother who was a schoolteacher. Welsing made sure to follow in both the footsteps of her mother and father, earning a Bachelor's degree at Antioch College and a Master's Degree at Howard University, where she became a licensed medical physician. A job that was very rare among black people during that time. A license in which she used to benefit the well-being of her people. Dr. Welsing's worth was one of education, in that she fed the people throughout her lifetime, knowledge of self.

This is very important, because we know if it's one thing the system of white supremacy hates more than the militant black man or woman, it's one who is feeding the masses knowledge of self and breaking the psychological chains from their mind. She is best known for her book the Isis Papers which theorized and analyzed the nature of white supremacy, breaking down key insight into this global system of white supremacy and how it is used to dominate and control us. Dr. Welsing, was one of the very few black Psychiatrists who was committed to her people, sacrificing all of her money and time to empower her people. The Isis Papers will forever be a classic and will always be remembered as one of the groundbreaking books in the conscious community.

Angela Davis 1944 –

Born in Birmingham, Alabama, to a father who was a service station owner and a mother who was a teacher, Angela Davis saw racism at a young age. Growing up in a section of Birmingham called Dynamite Hill, because so many homes in the area had been bombed over the years by the KKK. To make matters worse her mother was a member of the NAACP, when it was dangerous to be so open. As a teenager, she moved with her mother up to New York, where Davis graduated from Brandeis University Magna Cumlaude. Yet she never lost touch with the struggle, especially in the south. Davis, even before her graduation, was so moved by the death of the four little girls and the bombing of the Sixteenth Street Baptist Church in her hometown, she headed to join the Civil Rights Movement. Joining the Student Nonviolent Coordinating Committee and the Black Panther Party, all while earning her master's degree from the University of California at San Diego.

Davis became an activist for black equality and other things, such as approval in prison conditions. On August 7, 1970 in an attempted jail escape, that ended up with Superior Court Judge Harold Haley and three others dead, left Davis on the hot seat. Although she did not participate in the actual break out attempt, she became a suspect when it was discovered that the guns used by Jackson the suspect, was registered in her name, which led to her fleeing and being on the FBI's most wanted list. After several months, she was finally captured and put on trial for murder. It was thought as a sure conviction since she was seen by the dominant society as a black radical woman, who was a part of a black terrorist group.

Not only that, but she was to be extradited back to the state of California, where she could be executed. Yet this did not stop her from being unapologetically African. Coming to the court room every day of the trial, with an afro and putting her fist in the air so the camera could see. As well, she handled her own defenses, speaking for herself and bringing forth sufficient and overwhelming evidence that led to her acquittal, instantly making her an icon for Black Liberation, not just in the United States, but around the world as letters poured in from around the globe, making her a testament to what the black woman could do.

<u>Conclusion</u>

In conclusion I hope you understand by now that the black woman is special, a god on earth. Therefore, she must be loved, cherished, and appreciated to the highest standards. We must never disrespect her, nor should we tolerate any disrespect towards her from other communities. As well, it is an obligation that you, the black woman, don't allow yourself to be disrespected. For the respect you show towards yourself, will set the mark for how the world will see and treat you.

It is my hope that this chapter has helped the black woman to know you have everything inside of you. You have the courage and strength of Queen Nzinga, Queen Kahina, and Queen Mother Harriet Tubman. You have the will and persistence like your ancestor Sojourner Truth and Ida B Wells. You have focus and patience to educate the masses as Septima Clark and Dr. Frances Cress Welsing did. You have the ability of a God because God is in you.

We are the children of you no matter what race we are. Therefore, I challenge people of any race reading this book, especially the black man, that when you see a black woman, you pay homage. I'm not saying you have to get on your knees and kiss her feet. What I'm saying is you can call her Queen or God to remind her she is one. You can hold the door open for her or buy her flowers on a day other than Valentine's Day.

Carry her books to class or groceries in the house one day. These are ways you can pay homage. As a result, you will begin to see our relationship as black people grow, because as our black Queens grow, we as a community will too. Last but not least, if you don't learn anything else from this chapter my black queens know this, we love you, appreciate you and respect you sincerely. The world.

SOURCES

Part 1.

• Forbes, Jack D. Africans and Native Americans: The Language of Race and the Evolution of Red-Black Peoples. University of Illinois Press, 1993
• Revolvy, LLC. "Fugitive Slaves in the United States"
• Fugitive Slave Acts. History.com, A&E Television Networks, 27 Sept. 2018
• "PortCities Bristol" Slavery in Africa.
• Anderson, Claud. Black Labor, White Wealth: The Search for Power and Economic Justice. Duncan & Duncan, 1994.
• Fisher, Thomas. Negro's Memorial, or, Abolitionist's Catechism. Gale, Sabin Americana, 2012.
• Equiano, Olaudah, and Paul Edwards. Equiano's Travels: The Interesting Narrative of the Life of Olaudah Equiano or Gustavus Vassa, the African. Waveland Press, 2006.
• "History of the Holocaust" Holocaust Memorial Center.
• "Stono Rebellion (1739) | The Black Past: Remembered and Reclaimed" Redlining (1937-) | The

Black Past: Remembered and Reclaimed.
- "May 10, 1740 – South Carolina Enacts the Negro Act of 1740" Legal Legacy, 12 Apr. 2017.
- Bly, Antonio T. "Slave Literacy and Education in Virginia" Armistead, Lewis A. (1817–1863)
- Cartwright, Mark. "Slavery in the Roman World" Ancient History Encyclopedia, Ancient History Encyclopedia, 26 Sept. 2018.
- Smithers, Gregory D. Slave Breeding: Sex, Violence, and Memory in African American History. University Press of Florida, 2013.
- SUBLETTE, NED. AMERICAN SLAVE COAST: A History of the Slave -Breeding Industry. CHICAGO REVIEW, 2017.
- Simkin, John. Slavery in the United States. Spartacus Educational Publishers, 2014.
- Yee, Robert, and Kathryn Fuselier. "The Legacy of Slavery at Vanderbilt: Our Forgotten Past" Vanderbilt Historical Review, 17 Oct. 2016.
- Bennett, Dashiell. "The Ancestral Link Between the Bush Family and the Slave Trade Is Confirmed" The Atlantic, Atlantic Media Company, 29 Oct. 2013.
- Contributor, ABS. "9 White Celebs, World Leaders Whose Families Owned Slaves" Atlanta Black Star, Atlanta Black Star, 24 Aug. 2013.
- "Georgetown Apologizes for 1838 Sale of 272 Slaves, Dedicates Buildings" Georgetown University.
- Swarns, Rachel L. "272 Slaves Were Sold to Save Georgetown. What Does It Owe Their Descendants"? The New York Times, The New York Times, 16 Apr. 2016.
- Swarns, Rachel L. "Insurance Policies on Slaves: New York Life's Complicated Past." The New York Times, The New York Times, 20 Jan. 2018.
- "Fifteen Major Corporations That Profited From

Slavery" Loraine's Blog, 24 Jan. 2014.
- Crow, Jeffrey. "Slavery" Weapons in the War of 1812 | NCpedia, 2006.
- "The Amistad Case." National Archives and Records Administration, National Archives and Records.
- Contributor, ABS. "5 Slave Ship Uprisings Other Than Amistad" Atlanta Black Star, Atlanta Black Star, 12 Aug. 2015.
- Richardson, David. "Shipboard Revolts, African Authority, and the Atlantic Slave Trade" The William and Mary Quarterly, vol. 58, no. 1, 2001.
- "Slave Rebellions" History.com, A&E Television Networks
- "PortCities Bristol" Europe | The Places Involved | Slavery Routes | Bristol and Transatlantic Slavery | PortCities Bristol.
- "Haitian Revolution (1791-1804) | The Black Past: Remembered and Reclaimed" Redlining (1937-) | The Black Past: Remembered and Reclaimed.
- Ramsey, Kate. The Spirits and the Law: Vodou and Power in Haiti. The University of Chicago Press, 2015.
- Torin. "The Gilder Lehrman Institute of American History" Historical Context: The Global Effect of World War I | Gilder Lehrman Institute of American History.
- "Slavery The Real Story..." The Praetorian Writers' Group, 1 Sept. 2018
- "Patent Act of 1793".
- "Patent Act of 1836".
- "No. 127: Black Inventors." University of Houston
- WINSTONTIMES-DISPATCH, BONNIE V. "Jo Anderson" Richmond Times-Dispatch, Richmond Times-Dispatch, 6 Feb. 2013.
- "Slave Medicine" Thomas Jefferson, a Brief Biography | Thomas Jefferson's Monticello".

- "National Assessment of Adult Literacy (NAAL)" National Center for Education Statistics (NCES) Home Page, a Part of the U.S. Department of Education, National Center for Education Statistics".
- Coleman, Arica L. "Hidden Cost of Federal Recognition of Native American Tribes" Time, Time, 9 Feb. 2018.
- Siemaszko, Corky. "Sen. Mitch McConnell's Great-Great-Grandfathers Owned 14 Slaves, Bringing Reparations Issue Close to Home" NBCNews.com, NBCUniversal News Group, 9 July 2019.
- First Scholarship Fund, yaleslavery.org
- Slavery and Justice, Report of the Brown University Steering Committee on Slavery and Justice, Brown University.
- Crow, Jeffrey J. "Slavery" NCpedia
- Goodwine, Marquetta L. The Legacy of Ibo Landing: Gullah Roots of African American Culture. Clarity Press, 1998.
- Opala, Joseph A. The Gullah: Rice, Slavery, and the Sierra Leone - American Connection, Yale University.
- Abraham Lincoln's Letter to Horace Greeley
- "The Emancipation Proclamation" National Archives and Records Administration.
- Gienapp, and William E. "Abraham Lincoln and the Border States" Journal of the Abraham Lincoln Association, Michigan Publishing, University of Michigan Library, 1 Jan. 1992
- James M. McPherson, The Negro's Civil War (New York: Pantheon Books, 1965), Appendix A
- Ronald LF, Davis "Black Experience in Natchez: 1720-1880--Special History Study"
- Rogers, J. A. 100 Amazing Facts About the Negro with Complete Proof: A Short Cut to The World History of

The Negro. Wesleyan University Press, 2014.
- "African Americans and the Campaign for Vicksburg" National Parks Service, U.S. Department of the Interior.
- Magness, Phillip W., and Sebastian N. Page. Colonization after Emancipation: Lincoln and the Movement for Black Resettlement. University of Missouri Press, 2018.

- Kelly, Wisecup, African Medical Knowledge, the Plain Style, and Satire in the 1721 Boston Inoculation Controversy, Early American Literature, Vol. 46, No. 1 pp. 25-50, 2011

Part 2.

- Pruitt, Sarah. "Why the Civil War Actually Ended 16 Months After Lee Surrendered" History.com, A&E Television Networks.
- "Abraham Lincoln's Letter to Horace Greeley" Abraham Lincoln's Advice to Lawyers.
- Loewen, James W. "Five Myths about Why the South Seceded" The Washington Post, WP Company, 26 Feb. 2011.
- LII Staff. "13th Amendment" LII / Legal Information Institute, Legal Information Institute, 17 May 2018.
- Anderson, Claud. Black Labor, White Wealth: The Search for Power and Economic Justice. Duncan & Duncan, 1994.
- "Black Codes" History.com, A&E Television Networks.
- Costly, Andrew. "Southern Black Codes"

Constitutional Rights Foundation.
- CTI Review. "American Corrections" Google Books
- Banks, Cyndi. Punishment in America: A Reference Handbook. ABC-CLIO, 2005.
- Todd, William Andrew. "Convict Lease System" New Georgia Encyclopedia.
- Cable, George Washington. Grandissimes: A Story of Creole Life. Nabu Press, 2010.
- "The Convict Lease System by Frederick Douglass" The Meaning of July Fourth for the Negro by Frederick Douglass.
- Myers, Barton. "Sherman's Field Order No. 15" New Georgia Encyclopedia.
- Gates Jr., Henery Louis. "The Truth Behind '40 Acres and a Mule'" PBS, Public Broadcasting Service, 19 Sept. 2013.
- Waxman, Olivia B. "The History of Police in America and the First Force" Time, Time, 18 May 2017.
- Kappeler, Victor E. "A Brief History of Slavery and the Origins of American Policing" A Brief History of Slavery and the Origins of American Policing | Police Studies Online.
- Hartmann, Thom. "The Second Amendment Was Ratified to Preserve Slavery" Raw Story, Raw Story, 23 Feb. 2018.
- Smith, Sharon LaFraniere and Mitch. "Philando Castile Was Pulled Over 49 Times in 13 Years, Often for Minor Infractions" The New York Times, The New York Times, 21 Dec. 2017.
- Selk, Avi. "Gun Owners Are Outraged by the Philando Castile Case. The NRA Is Silent" The Washington Post, WP Company, 21 June 2017.
- Goodman, H. A. "Look at These Injury Photos of Darren Wilson. Did Michael Brown Really Possess 'Hulk

Hogan' Strength?" The Huffington Post, TheHuffingtonPost.com, 7 Dec. 2017.

- Bosman, Julie, et al. "Amid Conflicting Accounts, Trusting Darren Wilson" The New York Times, The New York Times, 25 Nov. 2014.

- Downs, Kenya. "FBI Warned of White Supremacists in Law Enforcement 10 Years Ago. Has Anything Changed?" PBS, Public Broadcasting Service, 21 Oct. 2016.

- TOBAR, HECTOR. "Deputies in 'Neo-Nazi' Gang, Judge Found: Sheriff's Department: Many at Lynwood Office Have Engaged in Racially Motivated Violence against Blacks and Latinos, Jurist Wrote" Los Angeles Times, Los Angeles Times, 12 Oct. 1991.

- Halloran, Liz. "Napolitano Apologizes, But Why?" NPR, NPR, 16 Apr. 2009.

- Wing, Nick. "We're Paying A Shocking Amount of Money for Police Misconduct" The Huffington Post, TheHuffingtonPost.com, 29 May 2015.

- Hee Lee, Michelle Ye. "Does the United States Really Have 5 Percent of the World's Population and One Quarter of the World's Prisoners?" The Washington Post, WP Company, 30 Apr. 2015.

- "Criminal Justice Fact Sheet" NAACP.

- Hee Lee, Michelle Ye. "Analysis | Giuliani's Claim That 93 Percent of Black Murder Victims Are Killed by Other Blacks" The Washington Post, WP Company, 25 Nov. 2014.

- "Crime in the United States 2013.

- "Violent Victimization Committed by Strangers, 1993-2010" Bureau of Justice Statistics (BJS).

- Redlining (1937-) | The Black Past: Remembered and Reclaimed.

- Bill Dedmen, "The Color of Money" The Atlanta Journal-Constitution, May 1, 1988.

- "Study Ties Loss of Jobs To Rise In Violent Crime" CBS Chicago, CBS Chicago, 30 Jan. 2017.
- A Pawn in the CIA Drug Game
- Freeway Rick Ross (1960-) | The Black Past: Remembered and Reclaimed.
- Grim, Ryan, et al. "Key Figures In CIA-Crack Cocaine Scandal Begin To Come Forward" The Huffington Post, TheHuffingtonPost.com, 7 Dec. 2017.
- Schou, Nick. "The Truth in `Dark Alliance'" Los Angeles Times, Los Angeles Times, 18 Aug. 2006.
- McVey, Austin "The 1989 NCCD prison population forecast: the impact of the War on Drugs" 1989.
- "UN Drug Summit: Undo a Decade of Neglect" Human Rights Watch, 17 Apr. 2015.
- LoBianco, Tom. "Report: Nixon's War on Drugs Targeted Black People" CNN, Cable News Network, 24 Mar. 2016.
- Campbell, John "Neoliberalism's penal and debtor states" 2009.
- Wagner, Peter, and Bernadette Rabuy. "Following the Money of Mass Incarceration" Prison Policy Initiative, 25 Jan. 2017.
- "US: America's Private Gulag" US: America's Private Gulag | Corpwatch, 1 June 2000.
- Peláez, Vicky "Global Research" 19 September 2018.
- Sloan, Bob. "Identifying Businesses That Profit From Prison Labor" PopularResistance.Org, PopularResistance.Org, 19 May 2015.
- Riley, Ricky. "13 Mainstream Corporations Benefiting from the Prison Industrial Complex" Atlanta Black Star, 31 Jan. 2017.
- Gao, George. "Chart of the Week: The Black-White Gap in Incarceration Rates" Pew Research Center, Pew Research Center, 18 July 2014.

- Guo, Jeff "America has locked up so many black people it has warped our sense of reality" 26 February 2016.
- Western, Bruce. Punishment and Inequality in America. Russell Sage, 2007.
- Lynch, Matthew. "High School Dropout Rate: Causes and Costs" The Huffington Post, TheHuffingtonPost.com, 2 Aug. 2014.
- Curry, Collen. "The Controversial Reason 1 in 13 Black Americans Can't Vote" Global Citizen, 6 Oct. 2016.
- Siemaszko, Corky. "Attorney General Sessions Heading to Epicenter of U.S. Opioid Epidemic" NBCNews.com, NBCUniversal News Group, 11 May 2017.
- Ingraham, Christopher. "Analysis | Drugs Are Killing so Many People in West Virginia That the State Can't Keep up with the Funerals" The Washington Post, WP Company, 7 Mar. 2017.
- Eyre, Eric. "Trump Officials Seek Opioid Solutions in WV." Charleston Gazette-Mail, 21 Nov. 2017.
- "West Virginia Has Highest Unemployment Rate among the States in August 2015" U.S. Bureau of Labor Statistics, U.S. Bureau of Labor Statistics, 25 Sept. 2015.
- Jacobs, Harrison. "Here's Why the Opioid Epidemic Is So Bad in West Virginia - the State with the Highest Overdose Rate in the US" Business Insider, Business Insider, 1 May 2016.
- Sussman, Anna Louie. "The Only State to Lose Jobs Since July Last Year: West Virginia" The Wall Street Journal, Dow Jones & Company, 21 Aug. 2015.

Part 3.

- Bump, Philip. "Analysis | Trump's Newest Travel

Part. 4

• Long, Edward. The History of Jamaica: Or, General Survey of the Antient and Modern State of that Island, with Reflections on its Situation, Settlements, Inhabitants, Climate, Products, Commerce, Laws, and Government, Volume II

• Harkless, Necia Desiree. Nubian Pharaohs and Meroitic Kings: The Kingdom of Kush. AuthorHouse, 2006.

• Fikes, Robert. "Kandake Amanirenas (?-10 BC)" Welcome to Blackpast •, 9 Sept. 2019,

• "Mitochondrial Eve" The Mitochondrial Eve: Have Scientists Found the Mother of Us All? MHRC.

• Catholic Online. "Hail Mary - Prayers" Catholic Online, Catholic Online.

• Mark, Joshua J. "Ma'at" Ancient History Encyclopedia, Ancient History Encyclopedia, 12 Nov. 2018.

• "The 42 Commandments of Ma'at" Lisapo Ya Kama, 20 Jan. 2018.

• "Out of the Darkness" Film

• Browder, Anthony T. From the Browder File: 22 Essays on the African American Experience. Institute of Karmic Guidance, 2000.

• "What Is Isis' Connection with the Throne?" Isiopolis, 14 Dec. 2013.

• "Tefnut." Pyramids of Ancient Egypt: Bent Pyramid of Sneferu, Dashur.

• Patrick J. Ryan, S.J. NAMING GOD: A QUANDARY FOR JEWS, CHRISTIANS AND

MUSLIMS. Spring McGinley Lecture, April 9-10, 2013.
- Full Text of "Passing", London: F. Warne; New York: Scribner, Welford, and Armstrong.

- Encyclopedia of Goddesses and Heroines" Google Books.
- "Muslim Identities" Google Books
- "Who's Who in Non-Classical Mythology" Google Books.
- Hubbard, Ben. "Saudi Arabia Agrees to Let Women Drive" The New York Times, The New York Times, 26 Sept. 2017.
- Hitti, Philip K. History of the Arabs: from the Earliest Times to the Present. Palgrave Macmillan, 2002.
- Healey, John F. The Religion of the Nabataeans: A Conspectus. Brill, 2001.
- Harris, Elise. "Who Is 'the Black Madonna' and Why Is She So Important?" Catholic News Agency, Catholic News Agency, 19 Dec. 2017.
- God. Merriam-Webster, Merriam-Webster.
- "Colostrum: Your Baby's First Meal" HealthyChildren.org.
- Wang, Wendy. "Interracial Marriage: Who Is 'Marrying out'?" Pew Research Center, Pew Research Center, 12 June 2015.
- NIGHTINGALE, EARL. STRANGEST SECRET. PMAPUBLISHING. COM, 2017.
- "Divorce Is Big Business" Hawaii Business Magazine, 15 May 2018.
- Howard, Caroline. "Elin Nordegren Walks With $100 Million" Forbes, Forbes Magazine, 9 Aug. 2011.
- Kirkwood, Thomas. "Why Women Live Longer" Scientific American, 1 Nov. 2010.
- McGuire, Danielle L. At the Dark End of the Street:

Black Women, Rape and Resistance - a New History of the Civil Rights Movement from Rosa Parks to the Rise of Black Power. Vintage Books, 2011.

- Brown, DeNeen L. "'I Have All the Guns and Money': When a Woman Led the Black Panther Party" The Washington Post, WP Company, 10 Jan. 2018.
- "Queen Mother Nana Yaa Asantewaa of West Africa's Ashanti Empire" Black History Heroes.
- "Women Leaders in African History: Ana Nzinga, Queen of Ndongo" The Met's Heilbrunn Timeline of Art History.
- "Dahia Al-Kahina & Askia Daud" When We Ruled *2nd Edition - 50 Greatest Africans - Queen of Sheba & King Sundiata.
- Harriet Tubman. Org
- "Sojourner Truth" Biography.com, A&E Networks Television, 27 Feb. 2018.
- "Ida B. Wells" Biography.com, A&E Networks Television, 19 Jan. 2018,
- "Clark, Septima Poinsette (1898-1987)" Boley, Oklahoma (1903-) | The Black Past: Remembered and Reclaimed.
- "Baker, Ella Josephine" Birmingham Campaign | The Martin Luther King, Jr., Research and Education Institute, 13 Dec. 1903.
- Welsing, Frances Cress (1935–2016)" Boley, Oklahoma (1903-) | The Black Past: Remembered and Reclaimed.
- "Dr. Frances Cress Welsing, Author of The Isis Papers, Dead at 80" Black Enterprise, 28 Sept. 2017.
- Davis, Angela (1944--)" Boley, Oklahoma (1903-) | The Black Past: Remembered and Reclaimed.
- Gottlieb, Karla. The Mother of Us All: A History of Queen Nanny, Leader of the Windward Jamaican Maroons.

Africa World, 2000.

• James, C. L. R. The Black Jacobins Toussaint L'ouverture and the San Domingo Revolution. Vintage Books, 1963.

Voice of the Ancestors

ABOUT THE AUTHOR

Chase McGhee is the author of the highly anticipated book series Voice of the Ancestors. He is a loving and caring family man and a committed member of the African American community, who has dedicated most of his young life to the freedom and liberation of his people. Chase is also the mentor of several African American students nationwide ranging from elementary to college school kids, with a focus on knowledge of self, economics, and anti-racism methods and strategies. As a result, making him one of the most influential and promising young African American leaders in years to come.

Made in the USA
Columbia, SC
24 July 2024

38680184R00113